Workbook 1

max maths

A SINGAPORE APPROACH

ALICE HANSEN DANIEL COLE
TONY COTTON DR BERINDERJEET KAUR

macmillan education
INTERNATIONAL CURRICULUM

Macmillan Education
4 Crinan Street
London, N1 9XW
A division of Macmillan Publishers Limited

Companies and representatives throughout the world

www.macmillanic.com

ISBN 978-1-380-01774-1

First published 2018

Page layout, illustrations and picture research by Star Publishing Pte Ltd
Cover design by Clare Webber
Cover illustration by Alan Brown/Advocate Art

Printed and bound in Brazil

2024
40

The authors and publishers would like to thank the following for permission to reproduce their images.

© **Royalty-Free**/Corbis p12(b)
© **Stockdisc Royalty Free Photos**/© Stockdisc Royalty Free Photos pp25(tr), 29(b), 65(t, b), 125(bcr), 162(tr), 173(r)
BANANASTOCK/pp110(t), 171(r, r, r), 172(r, r, r), 173(cl), 174(r, r, r)
BRAND X/pp4(flower), 5(flower), 9(flower, flower), 23(cl, bl), 49(bc), 88(tr), 95, 100(b), 106(t), 120(t), 123(t), 139(bm), 160(tr), 191(t), 200(tm)
Comstock Images/pp20(t), 99(b), 106(b), 152(bc), 173(bl)
CORBIS/pp2(t, tc, bc, br), 32(bc, b), 41(c), 99(bc) 101(t), 122(b, b), 155(t), 160(tml, br), 161(tl), 163(bl), 176(tcr), 197(r)
E+/Michael Phillips p156(t)
Eyewire/Getty Images pp9(rose), 63(tc), 76(t), 88(b), 139(br), 152(t), 196(t), 200(tl)
GETTY/pp4(butterfly), 5(butterfly), 14(tc, bc), 20(t, c), 24(t), 26(tl), 35(tl, tr), 41(t, b), 49(b, b), 52(tr), 53(tl, tr), 58(t), 61(tr, br), 63(bc, b, b), 74(t, c), 87(br), 90(tr), 110(b), 122(t), 123(b), 139(bcm), 146(t, t), 148(b), 150(t), 154(b), 160(tmr, tcr, bcmr, bcr, bl), 162(bl), 163(tr), 164(bc), 166(tl, tr), 168(tl), 169(tml, tmr), 170(t), 171(tl), 176(tl), 181(b), 182(t), 192(t), 194(tm), 195(b), 200(tmr), 201(tl), GETTY/Photodisc pp26(tr), 39(t), 149(t), 155(b)
Getty Images/iStockphoto Thinkstock Images/ajt pp63(t), 75(t), 160(tcml), Getty Images/eli_asenova pp61(tl), 171(bl), 194(tr), Getty Images/iStockphoto Thinkstock Images/BetaplusZ p150(b), Getty Images/iStockphoto/Thinkstock/Nikola Bilic pp58(b), 192(b), Getty Images/Thinkstock Images/Michael Blann pp49(t), 102(b), 145(t), Getty Images/iStockphoto Thinkstock Images/alexey_boldin p73(b), Getty Images/iStockphoto/Thinkstock/Charles Brutlag pp149(t), 164(tc), 177(tl), Getty Images/iStockphoto Thinkstock Images/Sascha Burkard p165(tl), Getty Images/iStockphoto Thinkstock Images/creisinger pp103(t, t), Getty Images/iStockphoto/Thinkstock/alejandro rodolfo dans p116(b), Getty Images/iStockphoto Thinkstock Images/Irina Drazowa-Fischer pp176(tcl), 177(bcl), Getty Images/EyeEm/Danielle Haasjes/EyeEm pp40(b), 85(tl), 172(cl), Getty Images/Hero Images/Hero Images p150(b), Getty Images/iStockphoto/Thinkstock/Jeff Huting pp147(t), 148(b), 198, Getty Images/Ingram Publishing Thinkstock Images/Ingram Publishing pp61(bl), 161(bl), 164(t), 194(tl), Getty Images/Hemera/Thinkstock/Pekka Jaakkola p152(tc), Getty Images/iStockphoto/Pavlo_K pp174(bl), 181(c), Getty Images/iStockphoto/Thinkstock/Janis Litavnieks pp23(t), 32(tl), Getty Images/iStockphoto/Thinkstock/Oleksiy Mark p160(bcl), Getty Images/iStockphoto Thinkstock Images/Alberto Masnovo p103(b), Getty Images/iStockphoto/Thinkstock/Michael Meyer pp4(bee), 5(bee), 165(tr), Getty Images/iStockphoto Thinkstock Images/IvanMikhaylov pp74(b), 120(b), Getty Images/iStockphoto Thinkstock Images/Bet_Noire pp162(tl), 193(t), Getty Images/iStockphoto Thinkstock Images/Ociacia p103(t), Getty Images/Dorling Kindersley RF/Thinkstock/Gary Ombler pp176(bl), 177(br), Getty Images/iStockphoto Thinkstock Images/Maksim Pasko p139(bl), Getty Images/iStockphoto Thinkstock Images/Picsfive p103(c), Getty Images Thinkstock Images/PhotoObjects.net p167(bl), Getty Images/iStockphoto Thinkstock Images/rambo182 p152(b), Getty Images/redmal p147(b), Getty Images/iStockphoto/tifonimages p65(tc), Getty Images/iStockphoto Thinkstock Images/ClaudioVentrella p191(b)
Image Source/pp14(t), 20(t), 48(chicken), 75(b), 148(b), Image Source/Frazer Cunningham pp85(tr), 172(tl), Image Source/www.imagesource.com pp66(t), 88(tl), 121(b), 139(bcr), 174(tl), 177(tr)
John Foxx Images/pp53(cl), 120(t)
Macmillan Publishers Limited/Paul Bricknell pp24(tcl), 40(t, tc, bc), 85(b), 89(t, t, t), 103(t), 149(t), 151(c, b), 160(bcml, bmr), 163(tl), 164(bl), 172(bl), 182(c), 195(tc), Macmillan Publishers Limited/Haddon Davies p174(cl), Macmillan Publishers Limited/Paul Bricknell/Dean Ryan pp23(br), 69(flowers), 200(t), Macmillan Publishers Limited/David Tolley/Dean Ryan p182(b), Macmillan Publishers Limited/David Tolley pp168(tr), 171(cl), 194(tmr)
Macmillan Australia/p148(t)
Macmillan Education/A Abierto Corazon/A Abierto Corazon p156(tc)
Macmillan Mexico/ Anna Godwin (Beehive Illustration) p176(br), Macmillan Mexico/Tony Sanchez p32(tr)
Photoalto/pp144(t), 161(br), 166(bl), 168(bl), 169(tl), 175(l)
Photodisc/pp4(flower), 5(flower), 9(sunflower), 13(tl), 22(t), 23(cr), 24(br), 25(tl), 48(t, tc, duck, lamb, cat, chicken), 49(tc, tc), 52(tl, cl), 53(cm, cr), 69(t, b), 86(t, t), 97(b), 98(toy car), 101(b), 144(b), 145(b, b), 149(b), 160(tl, tcml), 164(tl), 165(tm, bl), 169(tr), 170(cl, cl), 201(tmr), Photodisc/Creative Crop pp162(br), 167(r), Photodisc/Getty Images pp4(beetles), 5(beetles), 8(b), 22(c), 24(bcl, bcr, bl), 25(c), 35(tc), 48(chick, donkey, chick), 52(b), 72(b), 73(t), 102(b), 119(t, b), 125(bl, br), 139(bcl), 154(t, b), 156(bc, b), 164(bcr), 165(bm, br), 176(tr), 181(t), 193(b), 201(tml, tr), Photodisc/Getty Images/Don Farrall p154(c)
Photospin/p52(cr)
PIXLAND/Pixland pp154(t, c)
Stockbyte/pp24(tcr), 65(bc), 76(b), 99(c), 103(t), 125(bcl), 150(c), 151(b), 160(tcmr, stapler), 161(bml), 163(br), 164(br), 167(tl), 177(bcr), 195(t, bc)
STUDIO 8/pp14(b), 87(bl), 89(t), 90(tl), 98(tc)

Contents

Preface vi

1 Numbers up to 20 2
Practice 1: Counting to 10 2
Practice 2: Counting to 20 14
Practice 3: Place value 19
Practice 4: Comparing numbers to 10 22
Practice 5: Comparing numbers to 20 32
Practice 6: Order and patterns 38
Practice 7: Ordinal numbers 48

2 Addition to 20 56
Practice 1: Addition by counting on 56
Practice 2: Addition using number bonds 61
Practice 3: Adding by bridging to 10 73
Practice 4: Making and solving addition stories 85
Practice 5: Counting by twos, fives and tens 92
Practice 6: Estimating numbers to 30 95
Practice 7: Doubling and halving numbers 97
Practice 8: Doubling near numbers 100

3 Subtraction within 20 102
Practice 1: Subtraction by taking away 102
Practice 2: Subtraction by counting back 106
Practice 3: Subtraction using number bonds 110
Practice 4: Subtraction as 'how many more to make?' 116
Practice 5: Subtraction and addition word problems 118

4 Shapes and geometric reasoning 124
Practice 1: 2D shapes 124
Practice 2: Shapes and pictures 129
Practice 3: Grouping shapes 131
Practice 4: Patterns with shapes 135
Practice 5: 3D shapes 138
Practice 6: Recognising line symmetry 143

5 **Length** 144
Practice 1: Comparing the length of two objects 144
Practice 2: Comparing the length of more than two objects 147
Practice 3: Measuring length 150
Practice 4: Measuring length in units 154

6 **Mass** 160
Practice 1: Comparing masses 160
Practice 2: Measuring mass 170
Practice 3: Measuring mass in units 174

7 **Capacity** 176
Practice 1: Comparing capacities 176

8 **Time** 180
Practice 1: Reading a clock 180
Practice 2: Days of the week 185
Practice 3: Months of the year 185

9 **Money** 186
Practice 1: Coins 186
Practice 2: Exchanging money 188

10 **Data handling** 194
Practice 1: Reading and making pictographs 194
Practice 2: Reading Venn and Carroll diagrams 202

Preface

max maths Primary – **A Singapore Approach** is a mathematics course specially designed to meet the needs of learners following the **Cambridge Primary** curriculum framework in Stages 1 to 6.

The **Max Maths Primary** workbooks guide learners through key mathematical concepts, addressing the learning objectives in the **Cambridge Primary** curriculum framework. With plenty of scaffolded practice, the workbooks support the learning process at home and will help to further develop learners' enthusiasm towards learning.

Workbook features

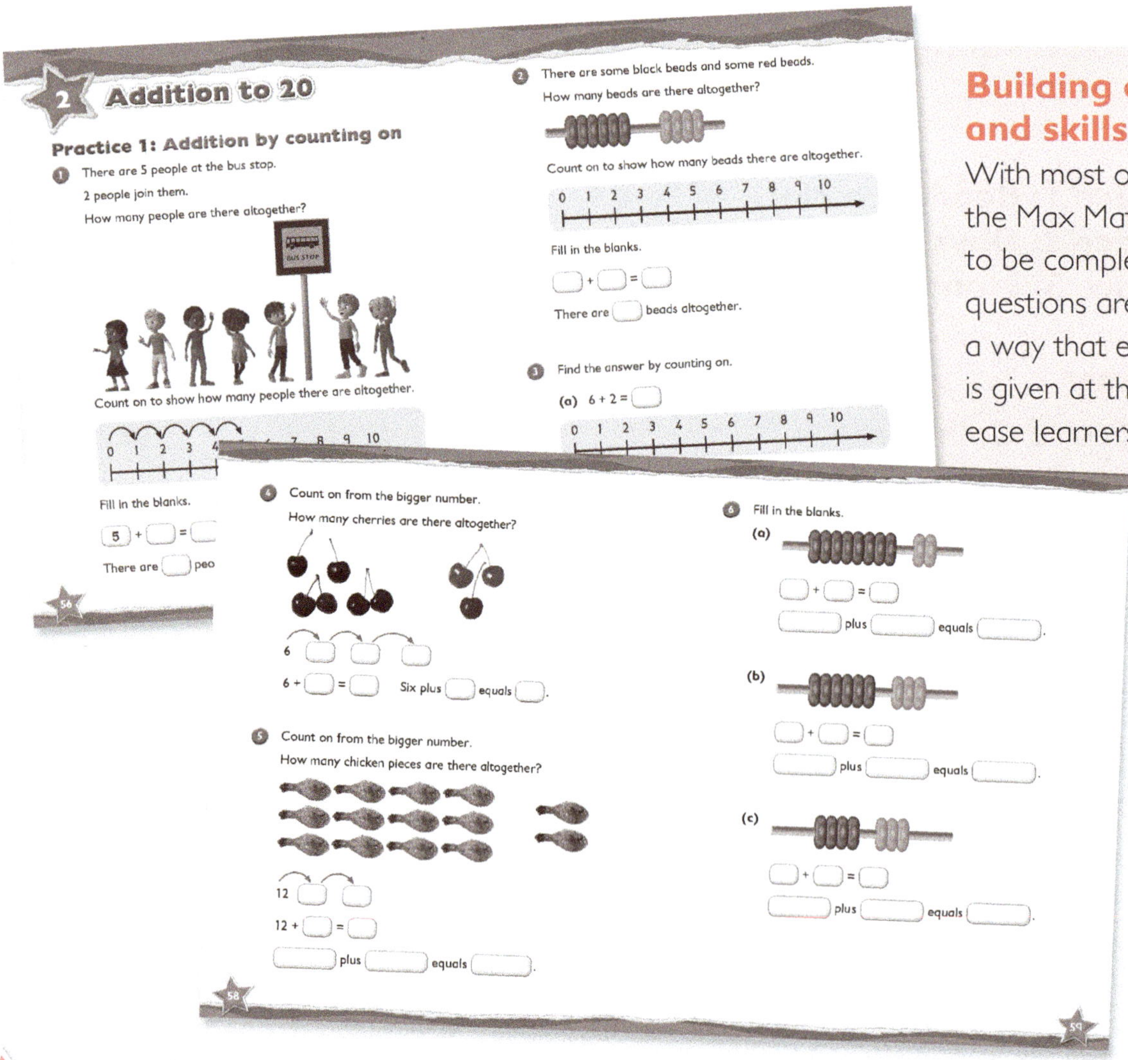

Building on concepts and skills

With most of the activities in the Max Maths workbooks to be completed at home, questions are scaffolded in a way that extra support is given at the beginning to ease learners into the task.

Engaging photographs and illustrations

Rich illustrations and photographs help to engage learners and encourage an enthusiastic approach to learning mathematics.

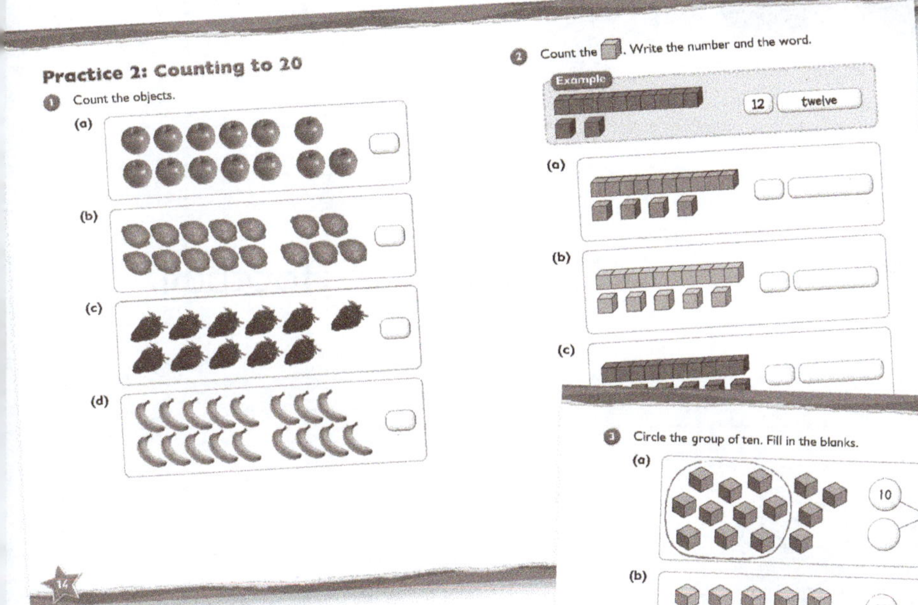
Practice 2: Counting to 20

1 Count the objects.

(a)

(b)

(c)

(d)

2 Count the ▯. Write the number and the word.

Example

12 twelve

(a)

(b)

(c)

Concrete, pictorial to abstract

Questions are graduated in a way that guides learners through the sequence from concrete, pictorial and abstract understanding of concepts.

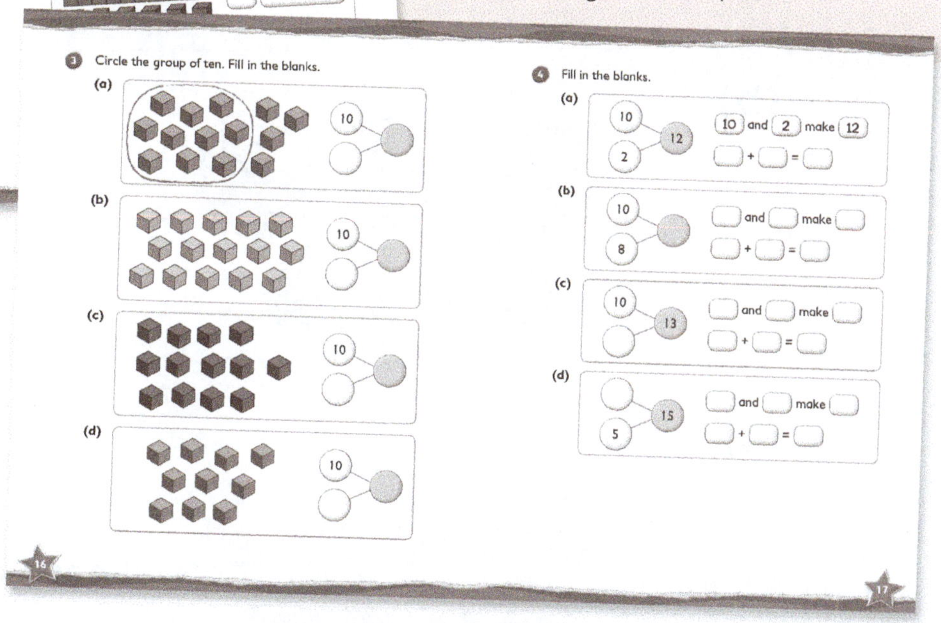
3 Circle the group of ten. Fill in the blanks.

(a) 10

(b) 10

(c) 10

(d) 10

4 Fill in the blanks.

(a) 10, 2, 12 — 10 and 2 make 12; ▯ + ▯ = ▯

(b) 10, 8 — ▯ and ▯ make ▯; ▯ + ▯ = ▯

(c) 10, 13 — ▯ and ▯ make ▯; ▯ + ▯ = ▯

(d) 15, 5 — ▯ and ▯ make ▯; ▯ + ▯ = ▯

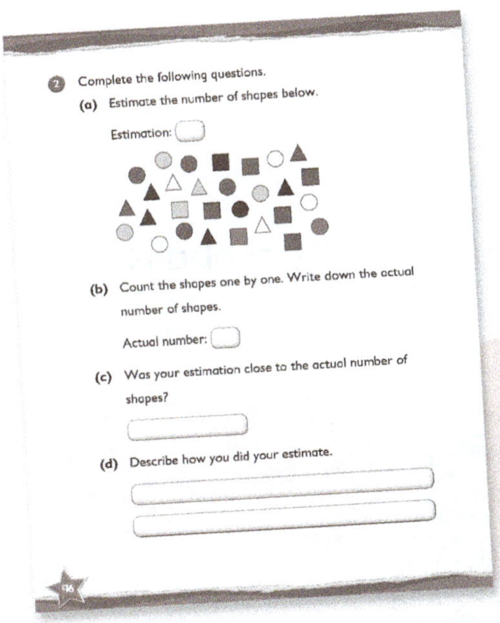
2 Complete the following questions.

(a) Estimate the number of shapes below.

Estimation: ▯

(b) Count the shapes one by one. Write down the actual number of shapes.

Actual number: ▯

(c) Was your estimation close to the actual number of shapes?

(d) Describe how you did your estimate.

Self-guided problem-solving

Problem-solving activities are embedded within practices for learners to combine knowledge of mathematics content and problem-solving skills.

1 Numbers up to 20

Practice 1: Counting to 10

1 Count the following items.

Example

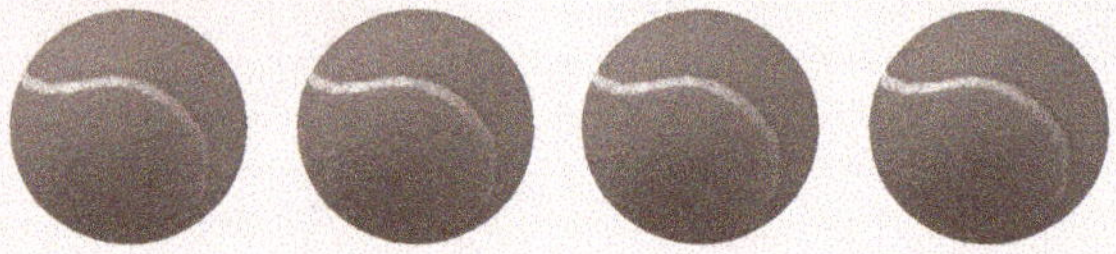

There are [4] balls.

(a)

There is [ ] football.

(b)

There are [ ] basketballs.

(c)

There are [ ] baseballs.

2 Count the dots.

Example

●●● There are 3 dots.

(a) ●●●●● There are ☐ dots.

(b) ●●●●●● There are ☐ dots.

(c) ●●● / ●●●● There are ☐ dots.

(d) ●●●●● / ●●●●● There are ☐ dots.

3 Draw the dots.

Example

Draw 2 red dots. ●●

(a) Draw 4 blue dots. ☐

(b) Draw 6 yellow dots. ☐

(c) Draw 7 green dots. ☐

4 Count each type of flower and insect you can spot.

5

5 Count the dots. Match them to a number.

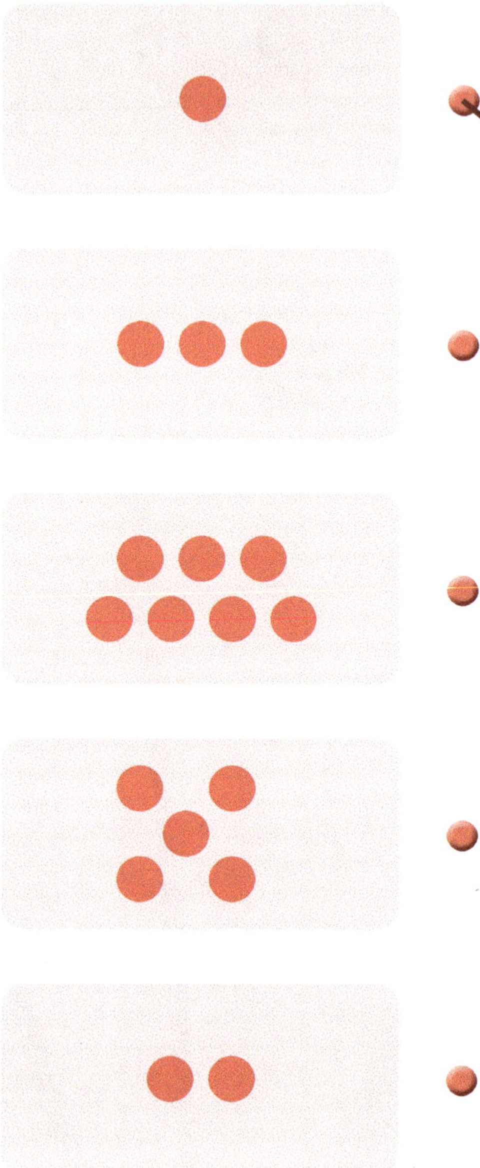

- 2
- 5
- 1
- 7
- 3

6 Match each word to the correct number of beads.

two

four

six

eight

nine

zero

five

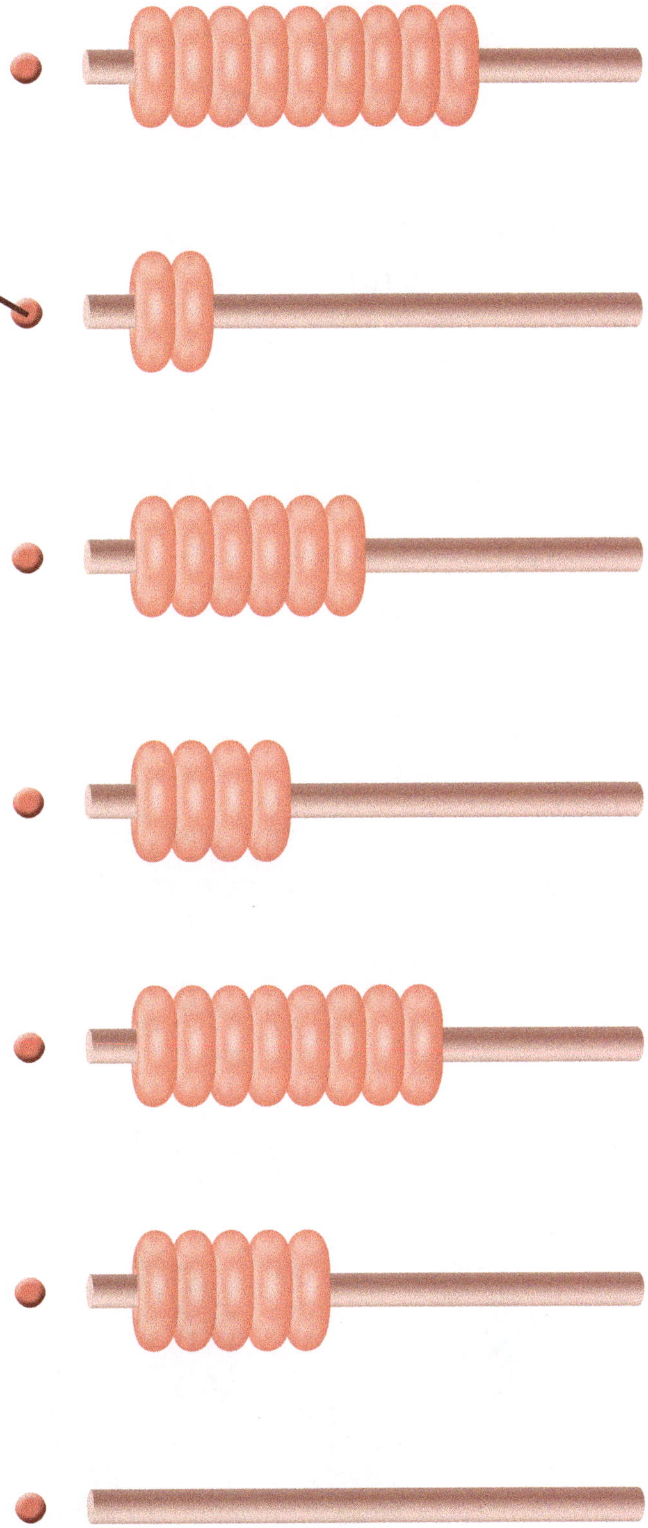

7 Read the words. Write the numbers.

Example

two [2]

(a) one [ ]

(b) five [ ]

(c) nine [ ]

(d) eight [ ]

(e) six [ ]

(f) four [ ]

(g) three [ ]

(h) seven [ ]

(i) zero [ ]

8 Count the ladybirds. Write the number in words.

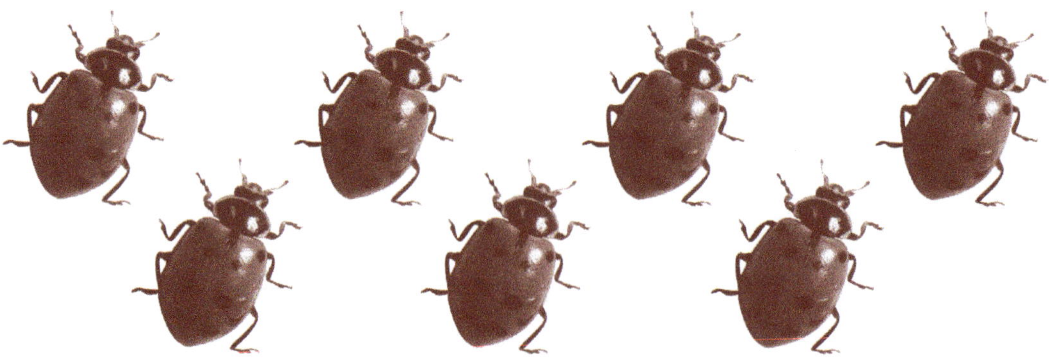

There are [ ] ladybirds.

9 Count the flowers. Tick the correct word.

(a)  ☐ two ☐ three ☐ zero

(b)  ☐ six ☐ seven ☐ five

(c)  ☐ five ☐ nine ☐ four

(d)  ☐ one ☐ zero ☐ three

(e)  ☐ three ☐ ten ☐ two

10 Fill in the blanks.

(a) one [ ]

(b) [ ] 2

(c) three [ ]

(d) four [ ]

(e) [ ] 5

(f) [ ] 6

(g) seven [ ]

(h) [ ] 8

(i) [ ] 0

(j) ten [ ]

11 Find, and circle, the numbers in the word search.

f	c	v	a	z	e	r	o
o	r	f	i	v	e	e	s
u	c	t	h	t	z	i	i
r	e	s	q	w	b	g	x
f	i	b	e	o	w	h	u
z	o	n	e	v	t	t	p
n	i	n	e	m	e	e	k
t	h	r	e	e	l	n	b

0 ~~1~~ 2 3 4 5 6 7 8 9 10

12 Write the words on the jigsaw pieces.

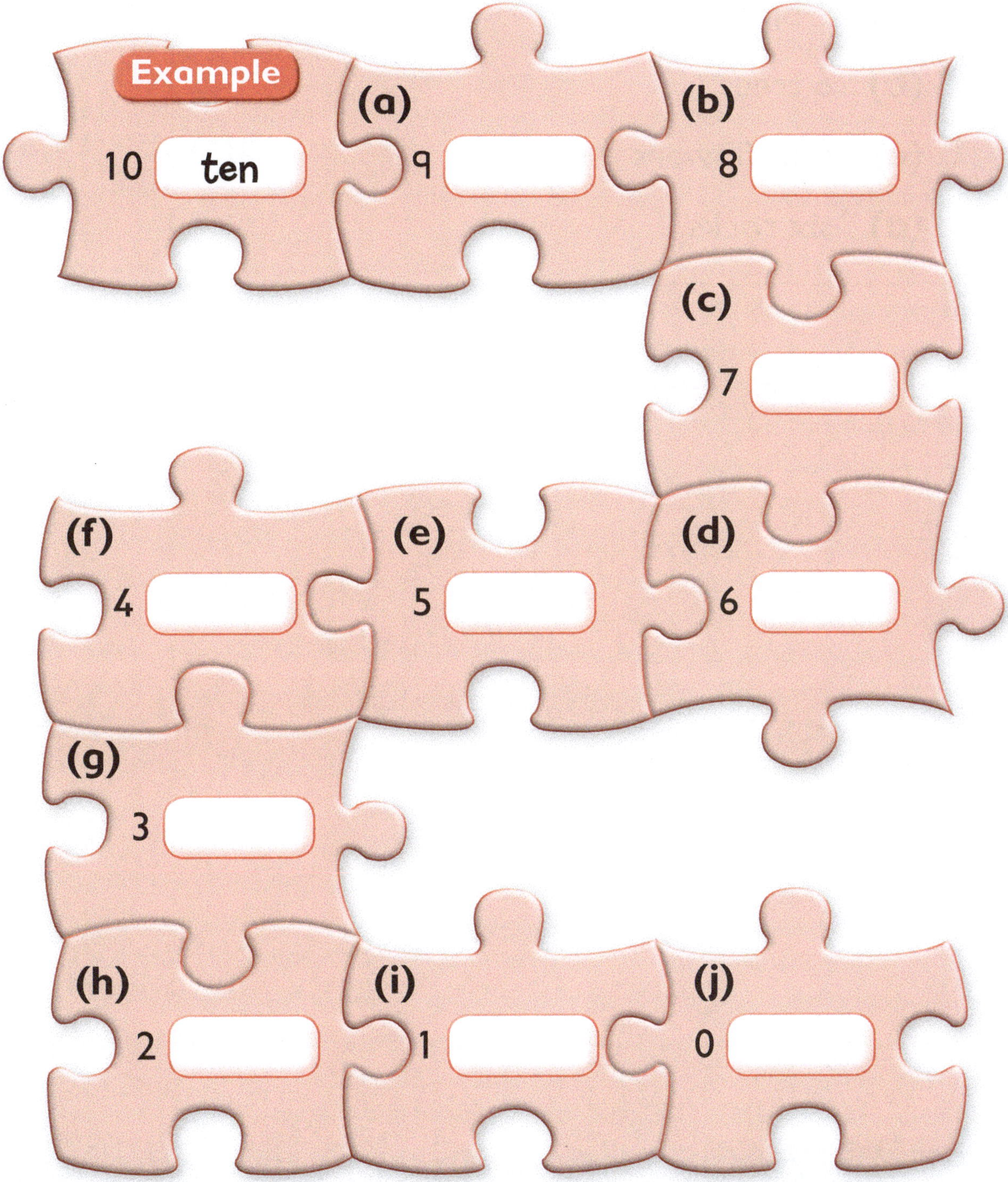

13 The jigsaw pieces form the shape of the number ____.

14 In the picture below, draw:

(a) 2 birds

(b) 6 trees

(c) four flowers

(d) six rocks.

15 Find the name of a place in the United Kingdom.

Match the number to the letter. Write the letter in the box.

r	d	m	a	b	i	e	c	g
0	8	2	3	4	7	9	1	5

	c	one
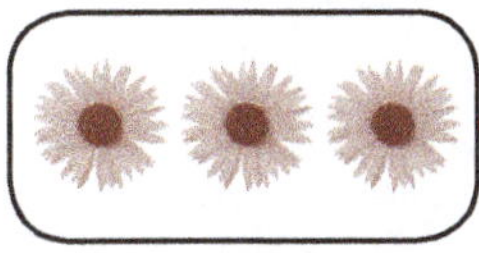		
		two
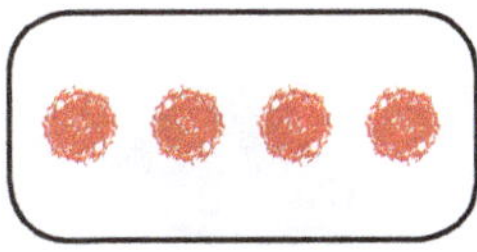		
		zero
seven		
		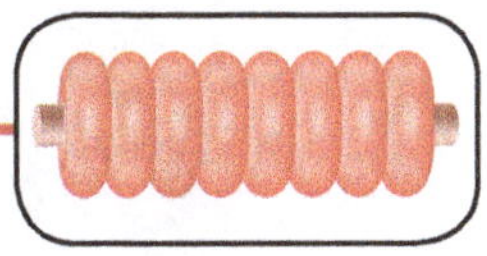
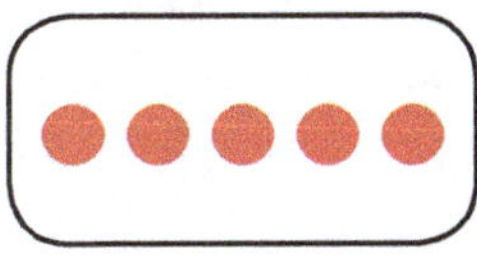		
		nine

Practice 2: Counting to 20

1 Count the objects.

(a)

(b)

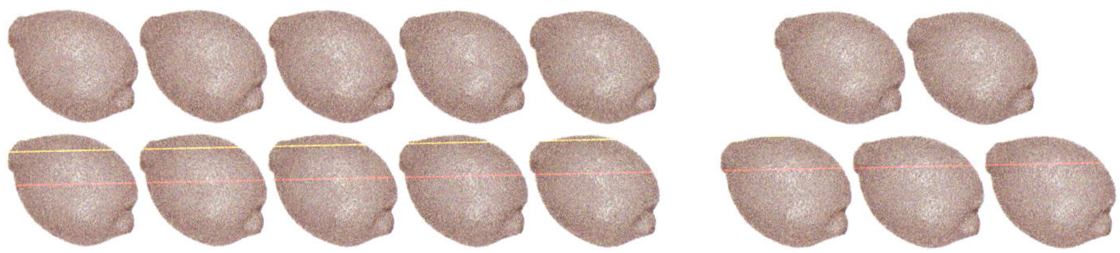

(c)

(d)

2 Count the 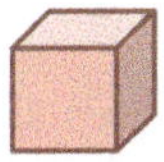. Write the number and the word.

Example

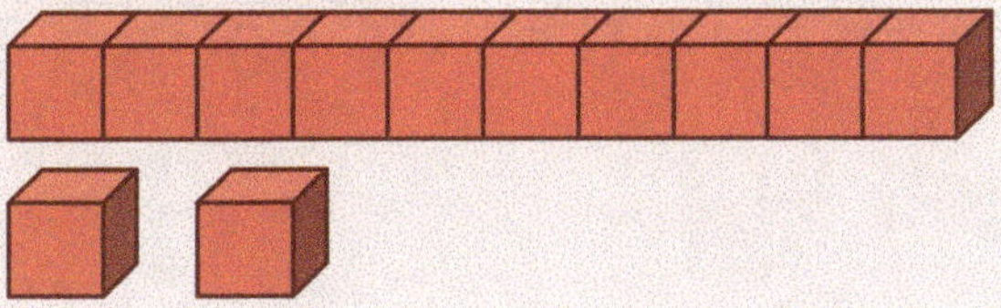

12 | twelve

(a)

(b)

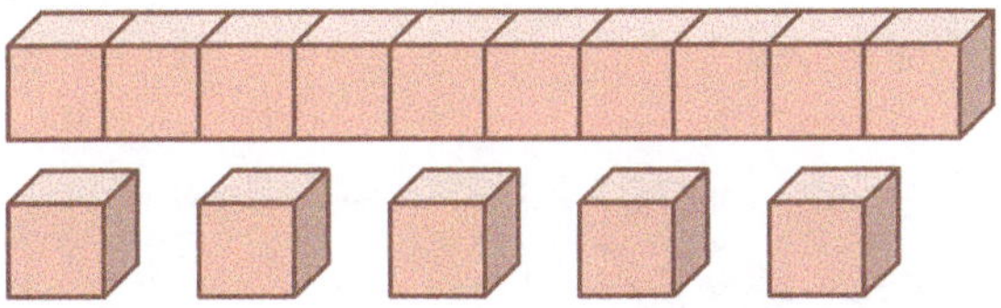

(c)

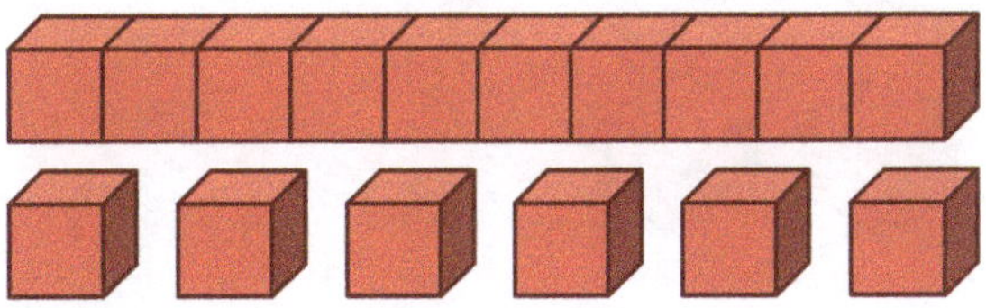

(d)

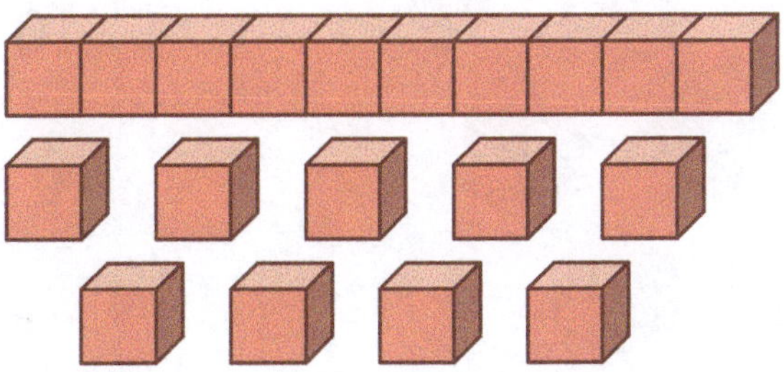

3 Circle the group of ten. Fill in the blanks.

(a)

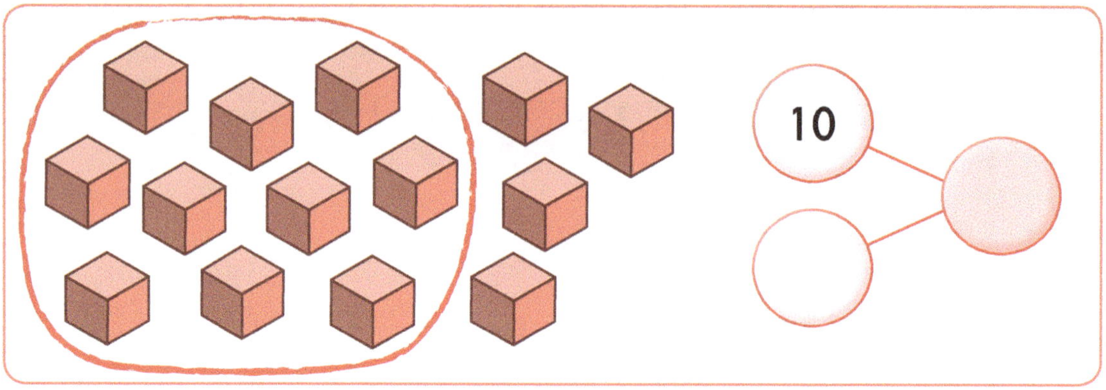

(b)

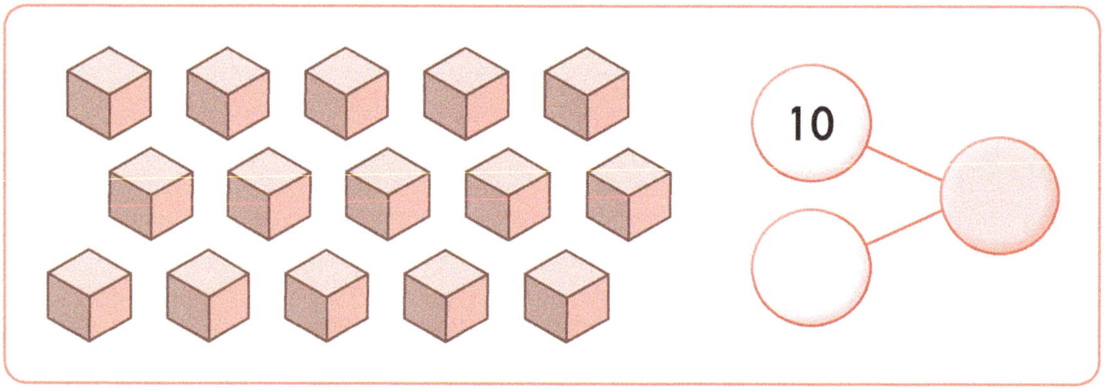

(c)

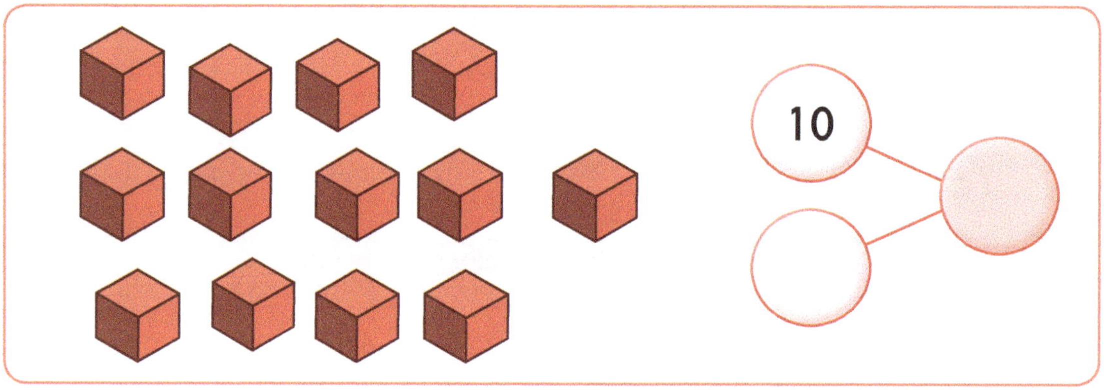

(d)

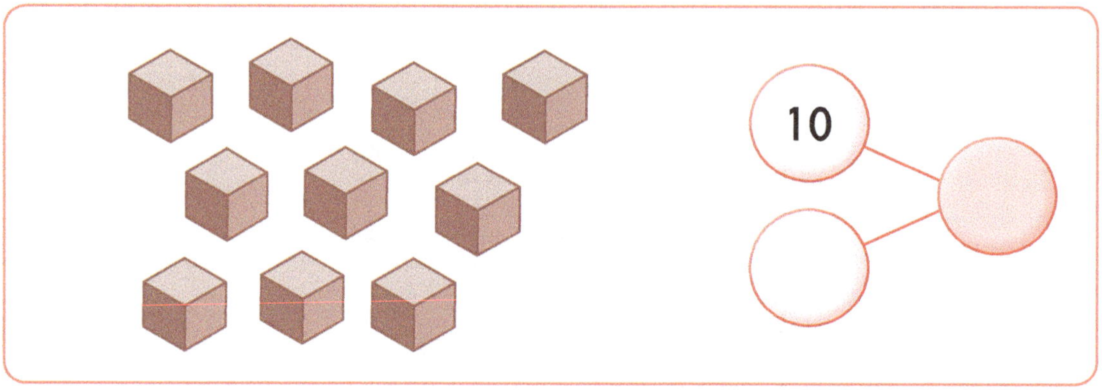

4 Fill in the blanks.

(a)

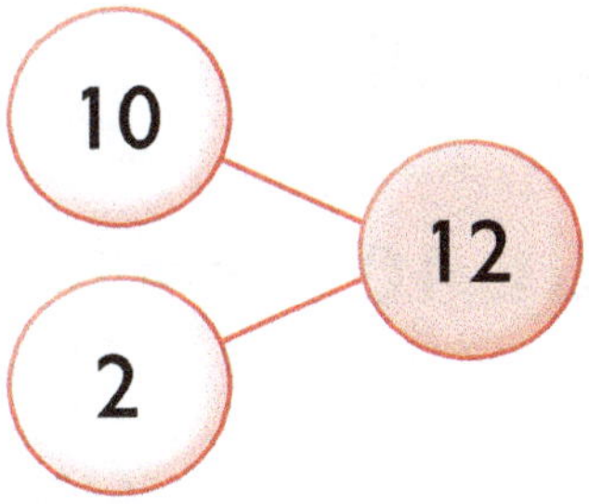

10 and 2 make 12

___ + ___ = ___

(b)

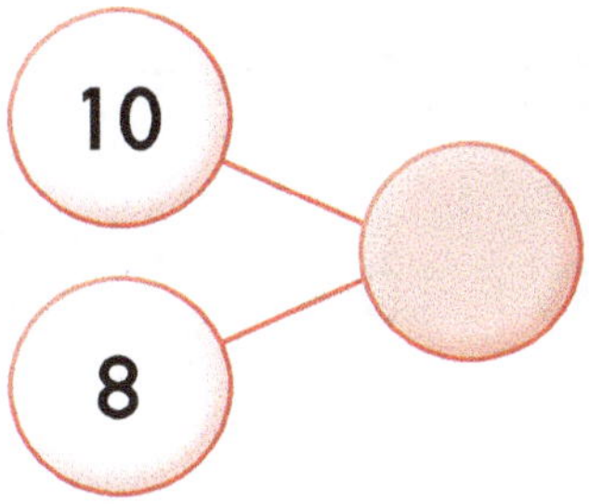

___ and ___ make ___

___ + ___ = ___

(c)

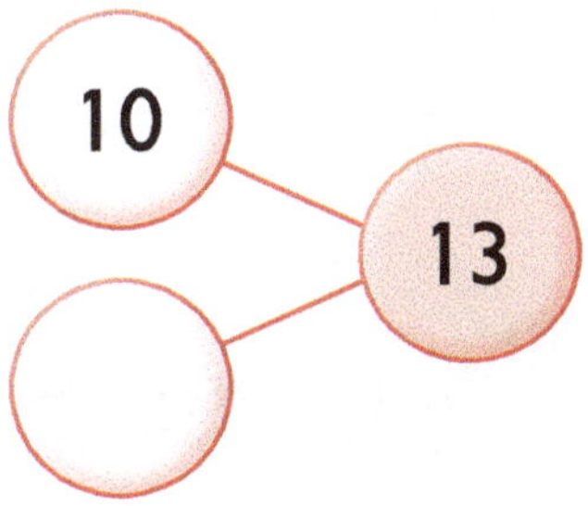

___ and ___ make ___

___ + ___ = ___

(d)

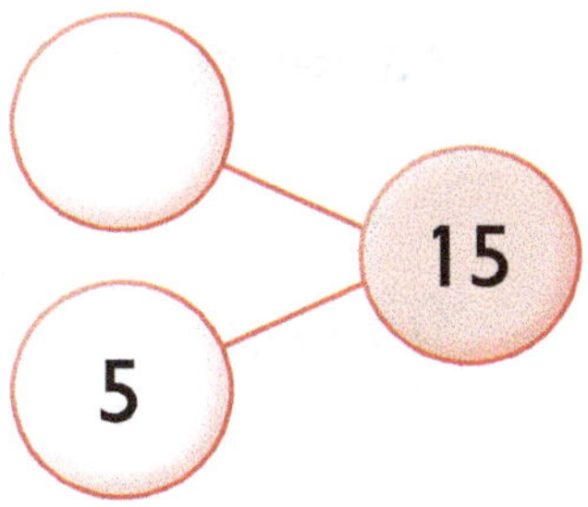

___ and ___ make ___

___ + ___ = ___

5 Fill in the blanks.

(a) 10 + ☐ = 11

(b) 10 + ☐ = 17

(c) ☐ + 10 = 12

(d) 10 + 9 = ☐

(e) ☐ + 6 = 16

(f) ☐ + 4 = 14

(g) 5 + ☐ = 15

(h) 10 + 0 = ☐

(i) 3 + 10 = ☐

(j) 10 + ☐ = 20

6 Match the number sentence to the answer.

Number sentence	Answer
10 + 3	13
10 + 5	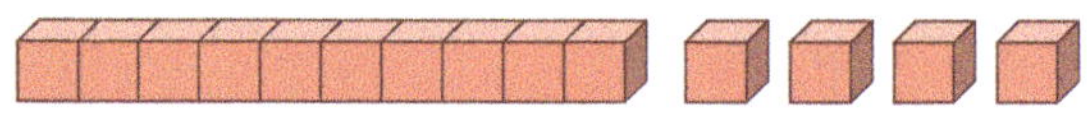
10 + 8	seventeen
6 + 10	fifteen
4 + 10	19
7 + 10	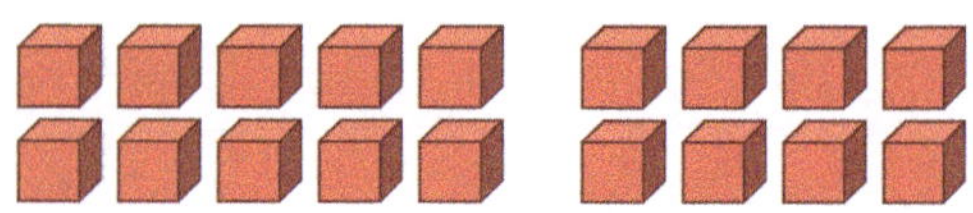
9 + 10	sixteen

Practice 3: Place value

1. Complete the following.

			Tens	Ones
Example		10 = 10 + 0	1	0
(a)	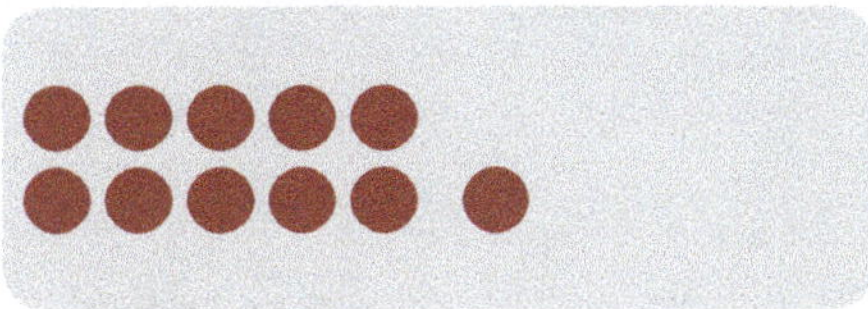	11 = 10 + ☐	☐	☐
(b)	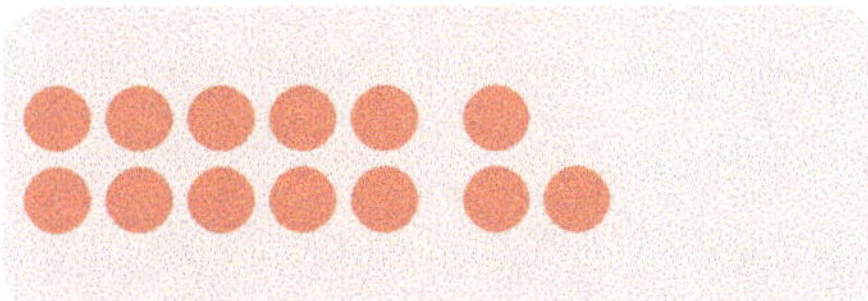	13 = 10 + ☐	☐	☐
(c)	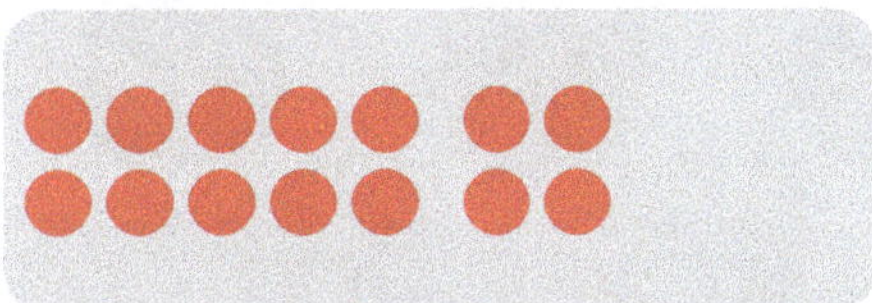	14 = 10 + ☐	☐	☐
(d)	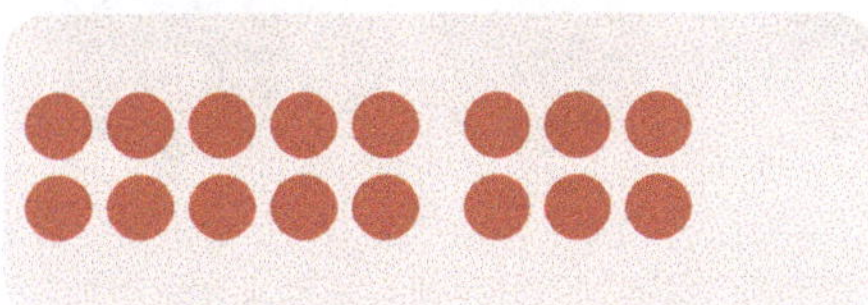	16 = 10 + ☐	☐	☐
(e)	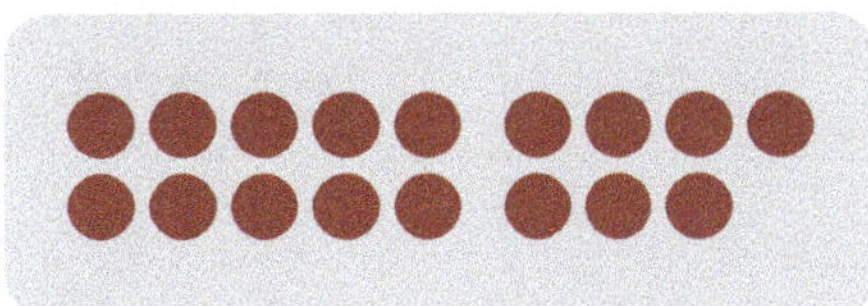	17 = 10 + ☐	☐	☐
(f)	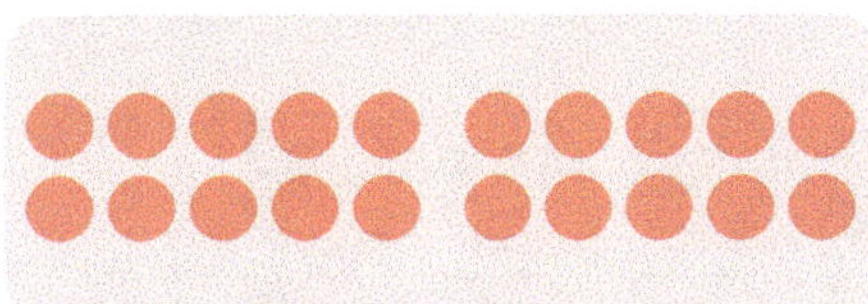	20 = 10 + ☐	☐	☐

2 Circle the group of ten. Fill in the blanks.

(a)

Tens	Ones

☐ = ☐ ten and ☐ ones

(b)

Tens	Ones

☐ = ☐ ten and ☐ ones

(c)

Tens	Ones

☐ = ☐ ten and ☐ ones

3 Fill in the blanks.

(a) 17

Tens	Ones

(b) 10

Tens	Ones

(c) 19

Tens	Ones

(d) 20

Tens	Ones

(e) 15

Tens	Ones

(f) thirteen

Tens	Ones

(g) fourteen

Tens	Ones

(h) sixteen

Tens	Ones

Practice 4: Comparing numbers to 10

1 Match the eggs to the chicks.

Circle the correct answer.

(a) How many eggs are there? 5 6 7

(b) How many chicks are there? 4 5 6

(c) Are the sets the same? yes no

(d) Are there more eggs or more chicks? eggs chicks

2 Count the bees. Count the flowers. Tick the set that has the same number of flowers as bees.

3 Circle the set that has **more**.

(a)

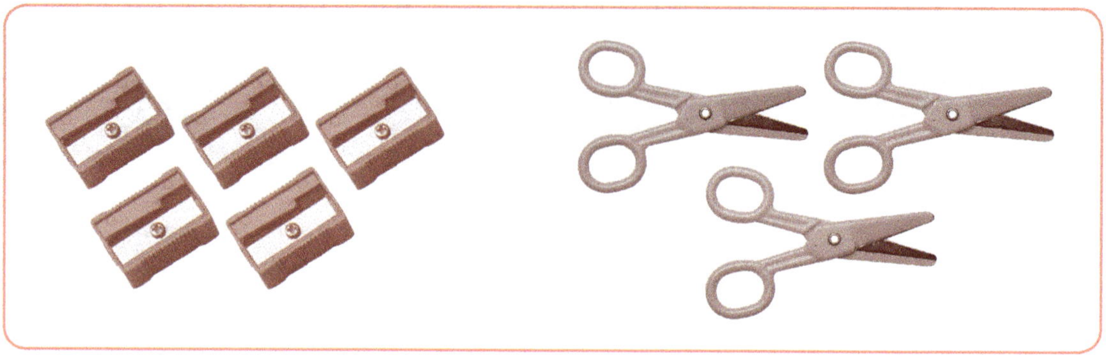

(b)

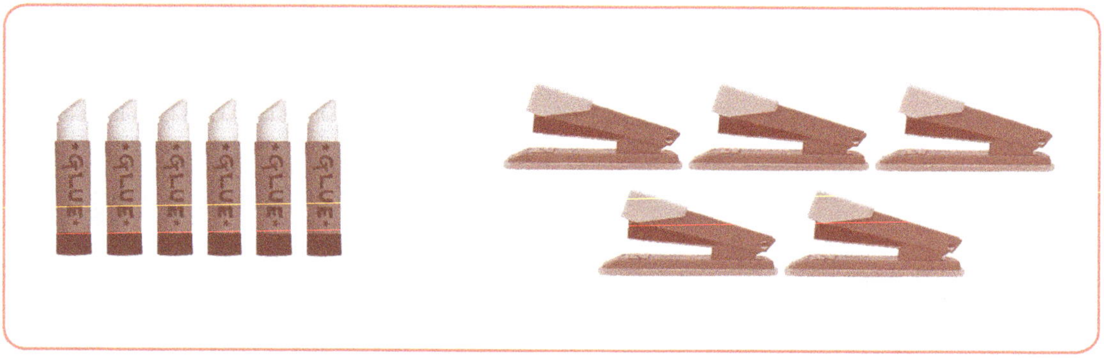

4 Circle the set that has **fewer**.

(a)

(b)

5 Look at the sets. Complete the sentences.

Example

pots

spades

There are more **pots** than **spades**.

There are fewer **spades** than **pots**.

(a)

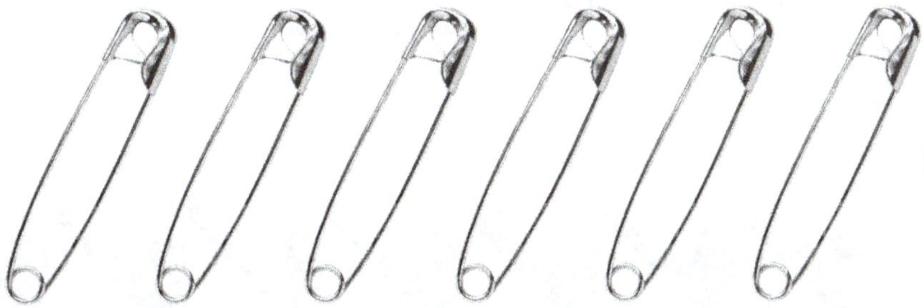

safety pins

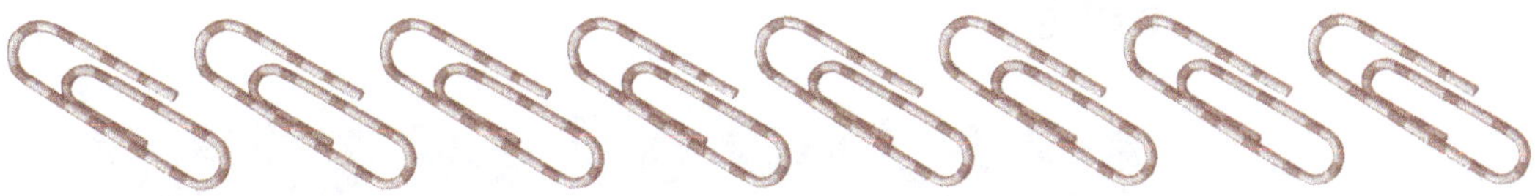

paper clips

There are more ____ than ____.

There are fewer ____ than ____.

There are 6 safety pins.

There are 8 paper clips.

(b)

sharpeners

pencils

There are more ____ than ____.

There are fewer ____ than ____.

(c)

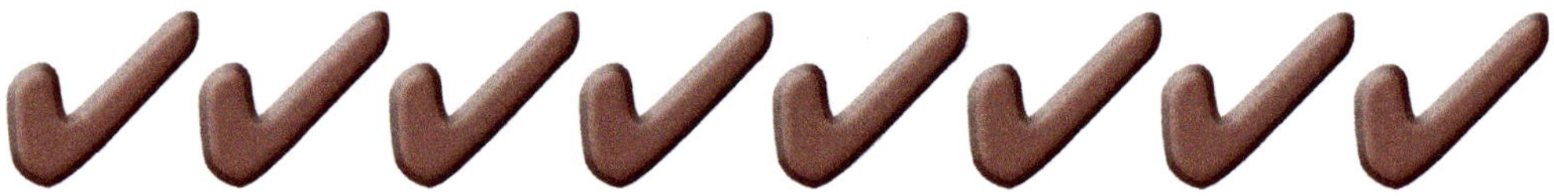

ticks

crosses

There are more ____ than ____.

There are fewer ____ than ____.

6 Look at the sets. Tick the correct sentence.

Example

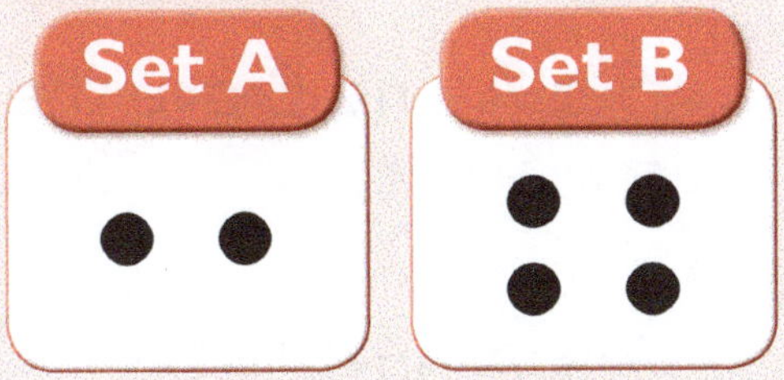

- [ ] Set A has more.
- [x] Set B has more.
- [ ] Set A and B are the same.

(a)

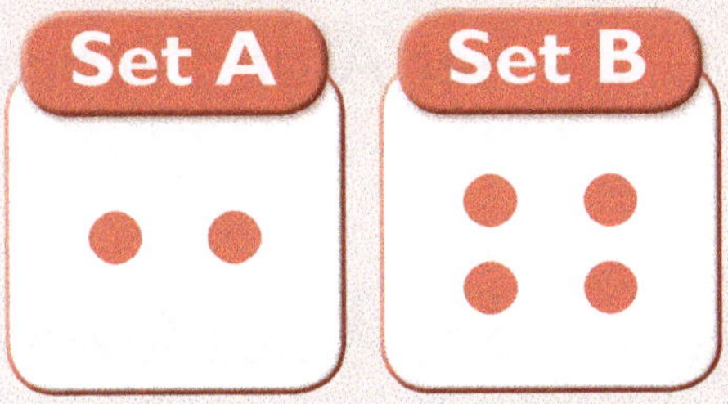

- [ ] Set A has more.
- [ ] Set B has more.
- [ ] Set A and B are the same.

(b)

- [ ] Set A has more.
- [ ] Set B has more.
- [ ] Set A and B are the same.

(c)

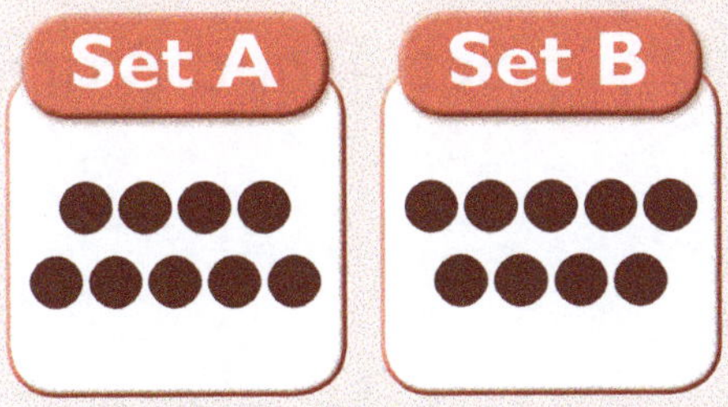

- [ ] Set A has more.
- [ ] Set B has more.
- [ ] Set A and B are the same.

(d)

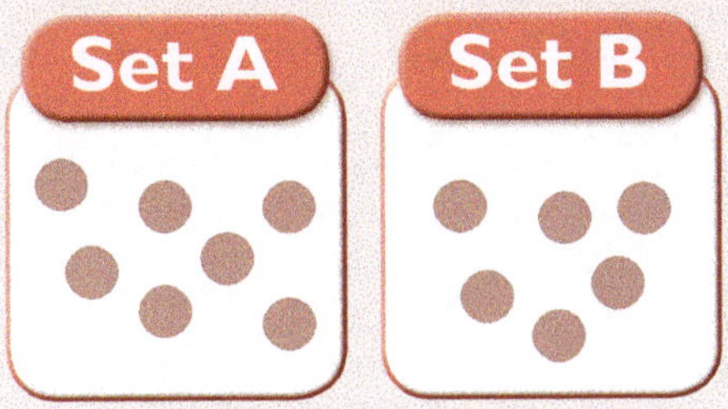

- [ ] Set A has more.
- [ ] Set B has more.
- [ ] Set A and B are the same.

(e)

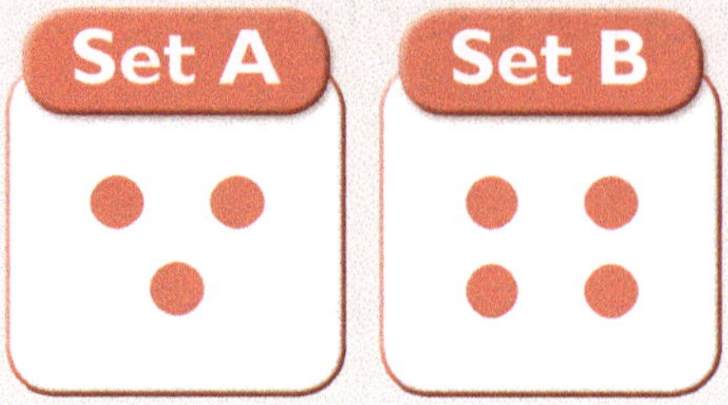

- [ ] Set A has fewer.
- [ ] Set B has fewer.
- [ ] Set A and B are the same.

(f)

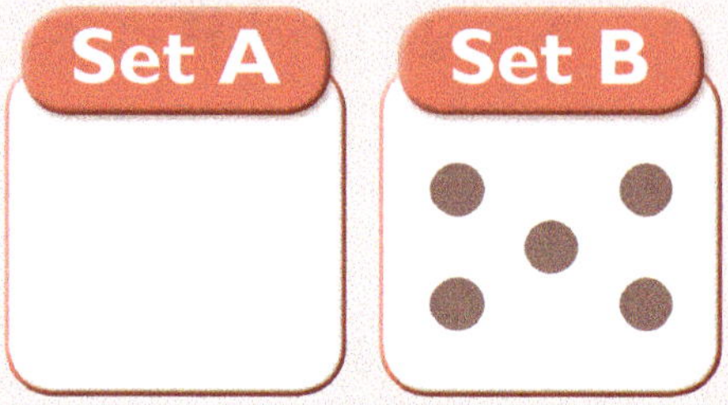

- [ ] Set A has fewer.
- [ ] Set B has fewer.
- [ ] Set A and B are the same.

(g)

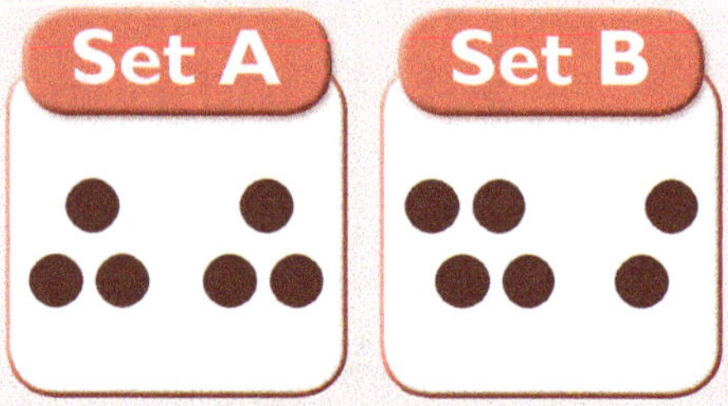

- [ ] Set A has fewer.
- [ ] Set B has fewer.
- [ ] Set A and B are the same.

(h)

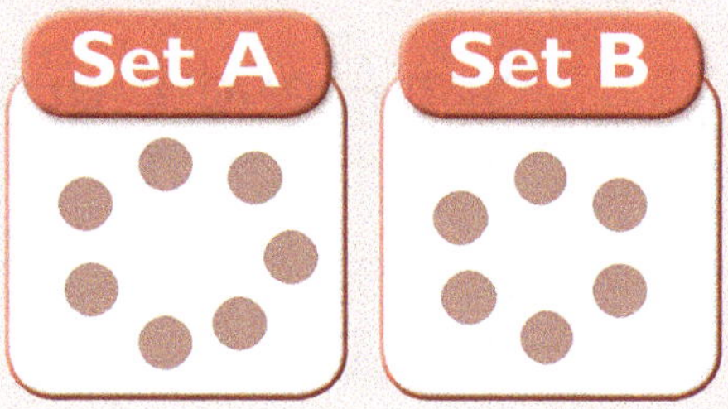

- [ ] Set A has fewer.
- [ ] Set B has fewer.
- [ ] Set A and B are the same.

7 Circle the smaller number.

(a) 4 5

(b) 0 2

(c) 3 1

(d) 8 9

8 Circle the bigger number.

(a) 7 9

(b) 5 3

(c) 1 0

9 Colour the word that is the bigger number blue or grey.

Colour the word that is the smaller number red.

Example

three	two

(a)

four	five

(b)

seven	six

(c)

one	nine

(d)

ten	eight

(e)

two	zero

10 Write the word 'bigger' or 'smaller' for each set.

Example

Set A	Set B
	four
bigger	smaller

(a)

Set A	Set B
	nine

(b)

Set A	Set B
7	six

(c)

Set A	Set B
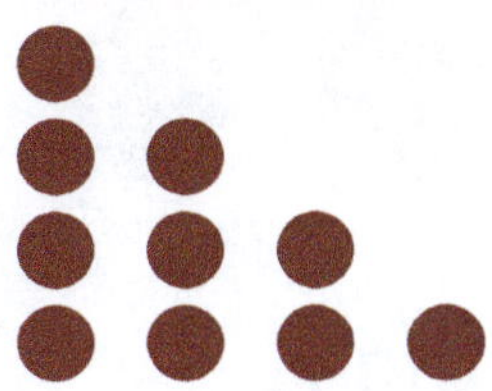	8

Practice 5: Comparing numbers to 20

1 Which set is bigger?

(a)

Set A

Set B

[ ] is bigger than [ ].

(b)

Set A

Set B

[ ] is bigger than [ ].

2 Count the objects in each set. Fill in the blanks.

(a)

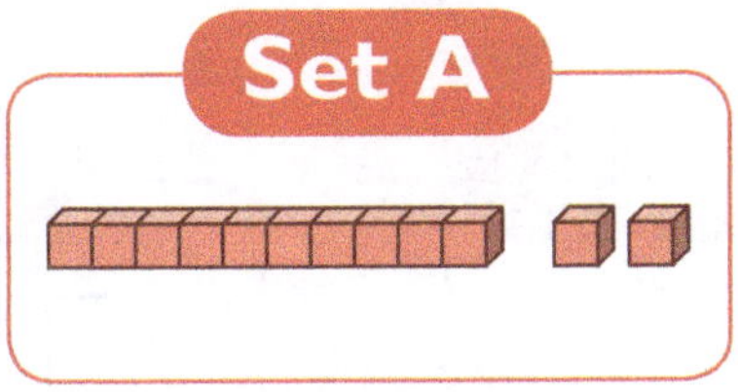

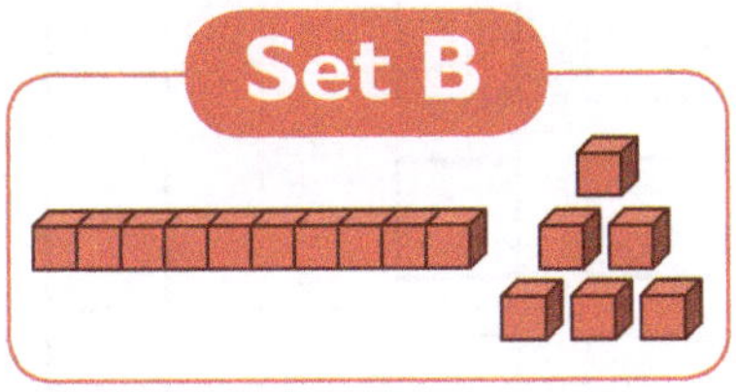

Set A is smaller than Set B.

There are 4 less  in Set A.

Set B is ________ than Set A.

There are 4 ________  in Set B.

(b)

Set A is ________ than Set B.

There is 1 ________  in Set A.

Set B is ________ than Set A.

There is 1 ________  in Set B.

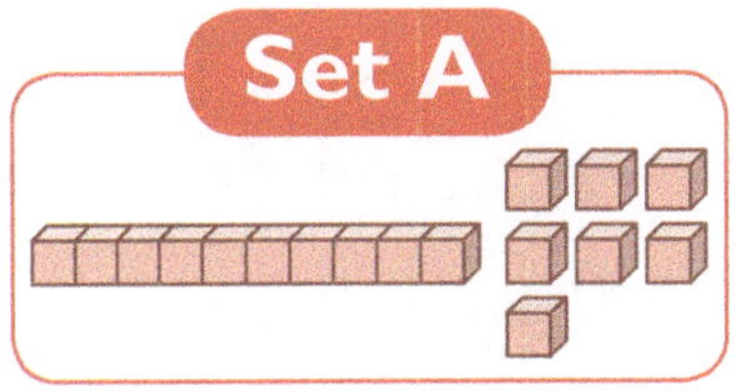

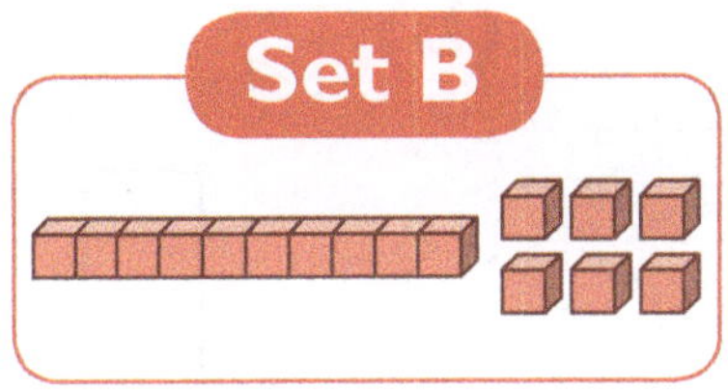

(c)

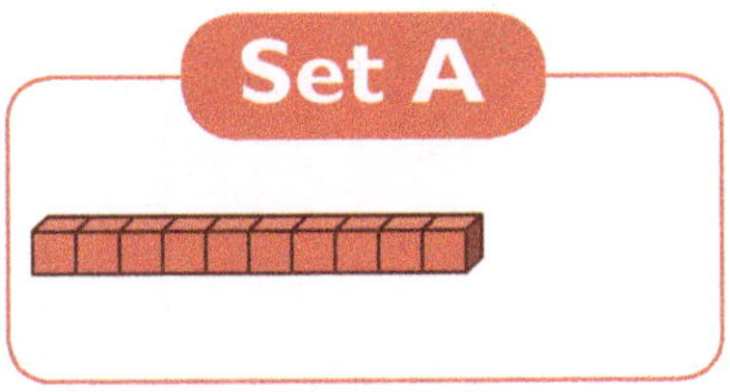

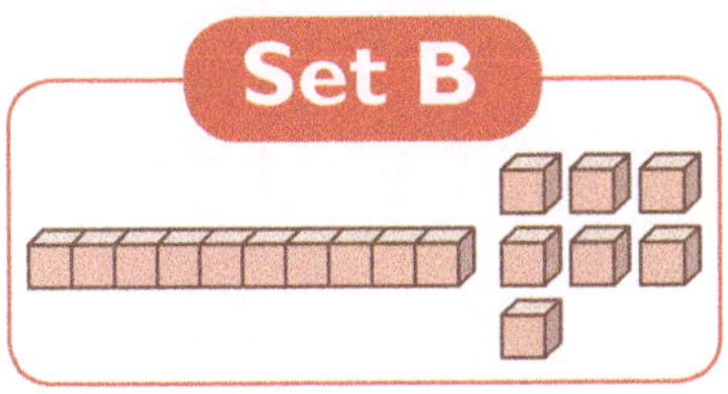

Set A is ________ than Set B.

There are 7 ________  in Set A.

Set B is ________ than Set A.

There are 7 ________ 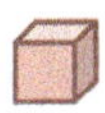 in Set B.

3 Count the objects in each set. Colour the biggest set red, and the smallest set blue.

(a)

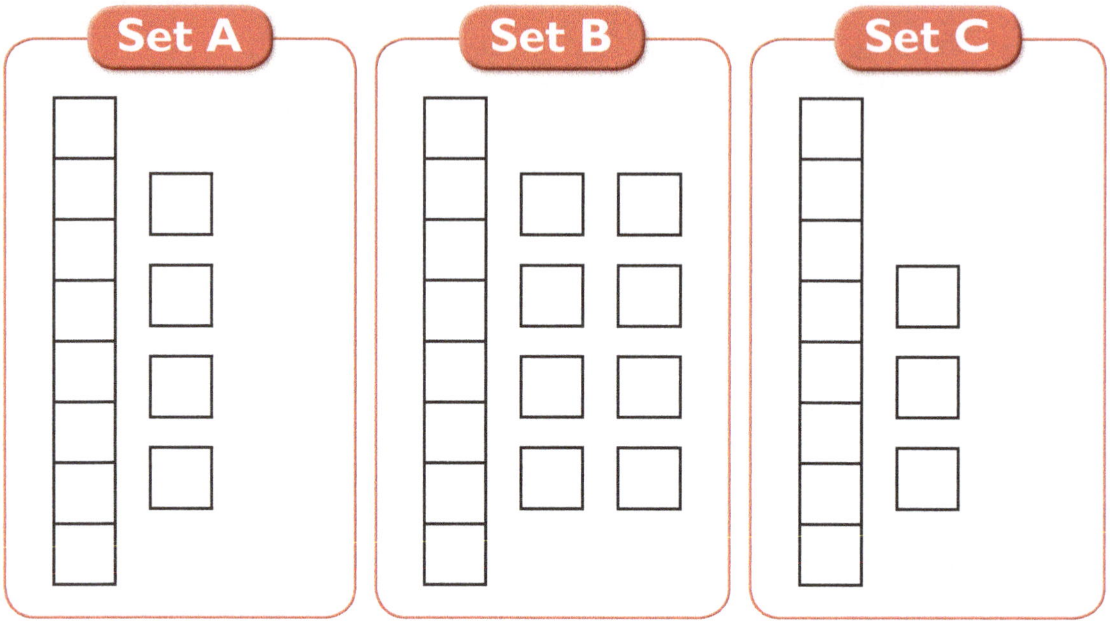

(b)

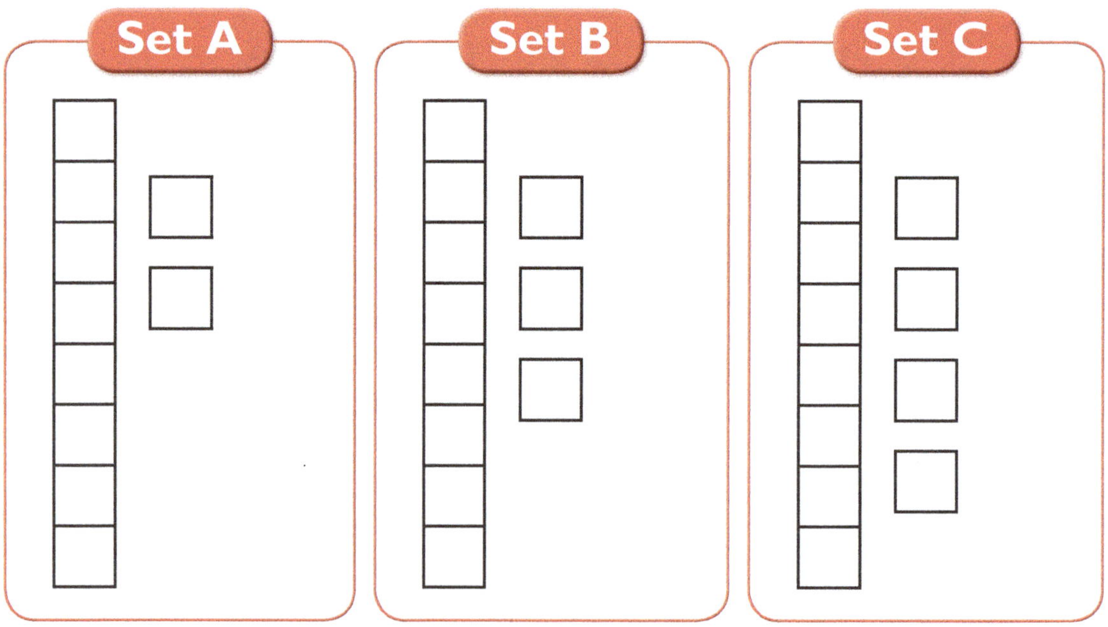

4 Count the objects in each set. Arrange the numbers from the biggest to the smallest and the smallest to the biggest.

Set A

☐ objects

Set B

☐ objects

Set C

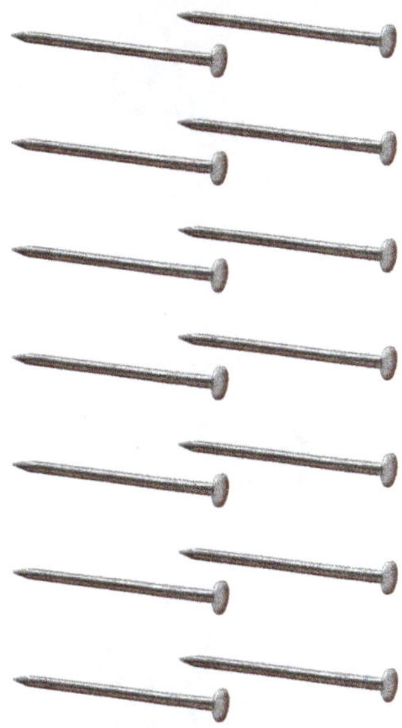

☐ objects

☐ → ☐ → ☐

biggest — smallest

☐ → ☐ → ☐

smallest — biggest

5 Arrange the numbers from the biggest to the smallest.

(a)

20 12 14

☐ → ☐ → ☐

(b)

18 19 17

☐ → ☐ → ☐

(c)

9 19 11 16

☐ → ☐ → ☐ → ☐

6 Arrange the numbers from the smallest to the biggest.

Complete the questions.

(a) 17 12 15 16

☐ → ☐ → ☐ → ☐

Which number is the biggest? ☐

Which number is the smallest? ☐

(b) 10 14 11 15

☐ → ☐ → ☐ → ☐

Which number is the biggest? ☐

Which number is the smallest? ☐

Practice 6: Order and patterns

1 Look at the numbers in the chain. Write the next number.

Example

3	4	5	6

(a)

6	7	8	

(b)

6	5	4	

(c)

1		3	4

(d)

10	9		7

2 Look at the pattern. Colour the missing beads.

Example

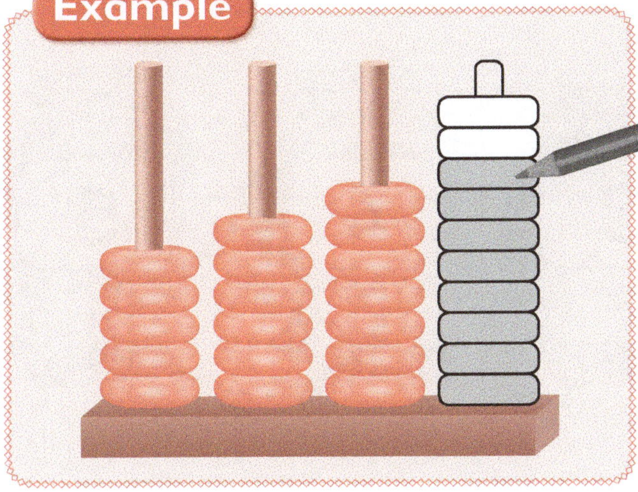

(a)

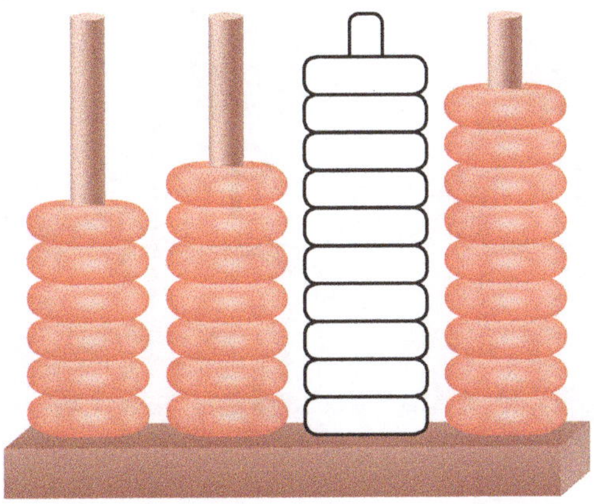

(b)

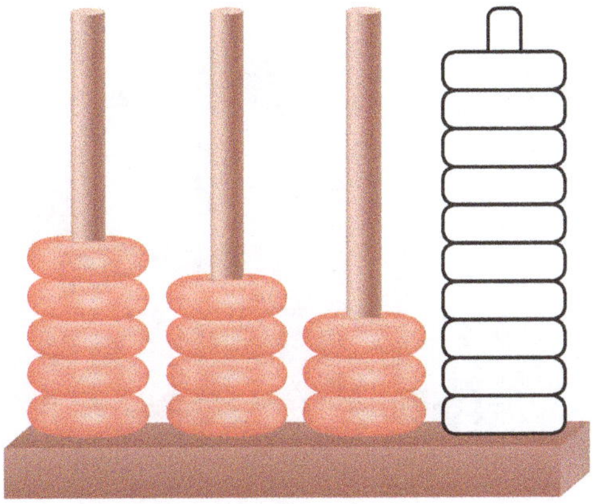

(c)

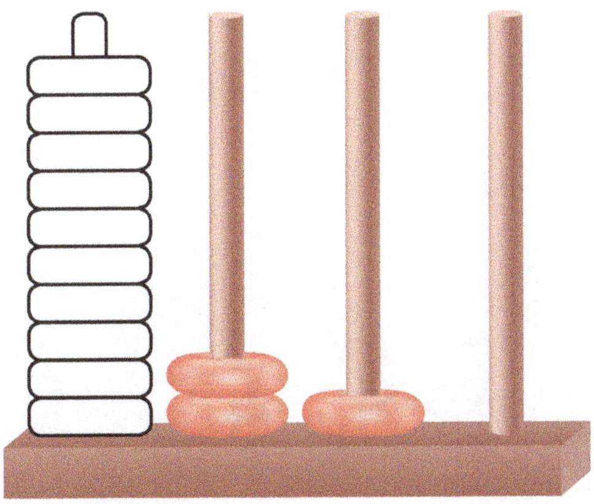

(d)

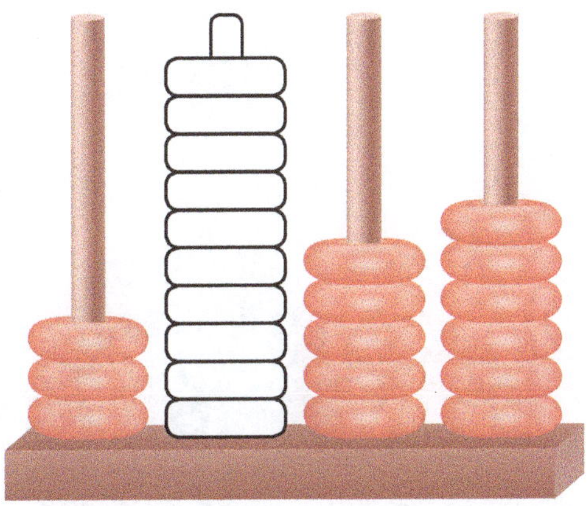

3 Write the next number in the pattern.

Example

(a)

(b)

(c)

4 Fill in the missing number in the pattern.

(a)

(b)

(c)

5 Complete the patterns.

(a)

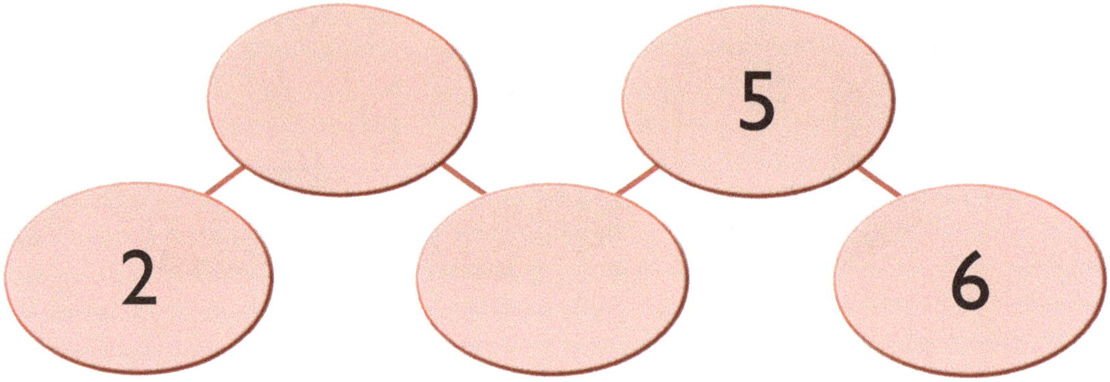

(b)

(c)

(d)

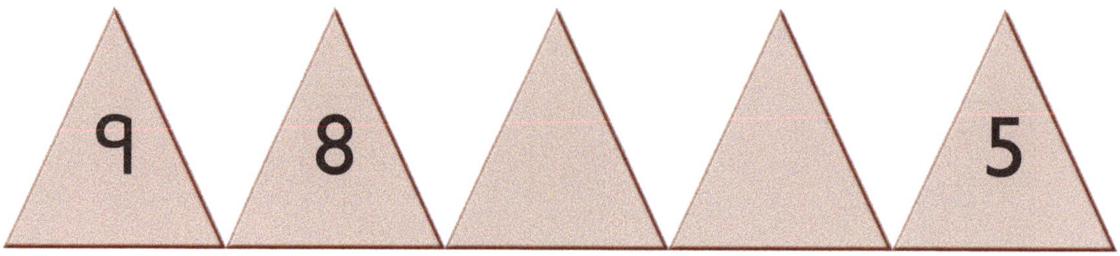

6 Complete the patterns.

(a) 6, 7, ☐, 9, ☐

(b) ☐, 1, 2, ☐, 4

(c) ☐, ☐, 5, 6, 7

(d) 10, ☐, ☐, 7, 6

(e) ☐, 4, ☐, 2, 1

(f) 8, 7, ☐, ☐, 4

7 Use the words in the box to complete the sentences.

more than	**less than**

Example

1 less than 5 is 4.

(a) 1 ☐ 2 is 3.

(b) 1 ☐ 6 is 5.

(c) 1 ☐ 1 is 2.

(d) 1 ☐ 8 is 7.

(e) 10 is 1 ☐ 9.

(f) 5 is 1 ☐ 6.

(g) 0 is 1 ☐ 1.

(h) 3 is 1 ☐ 4.

8 Tick the box for the blocks that come next in the pattern.

(a)

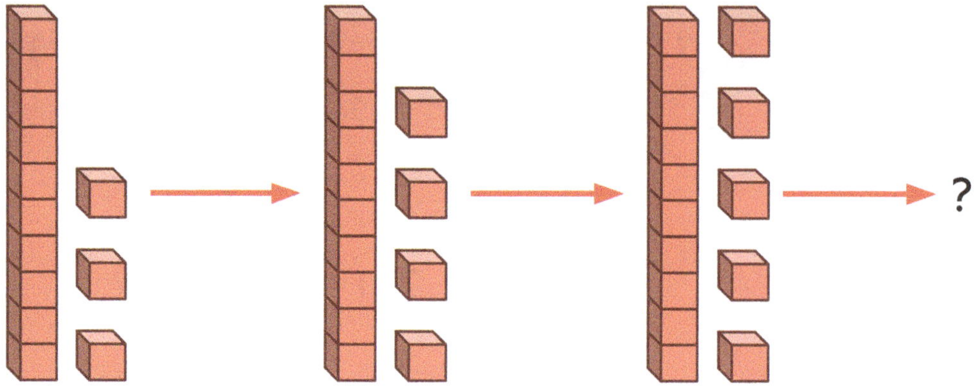

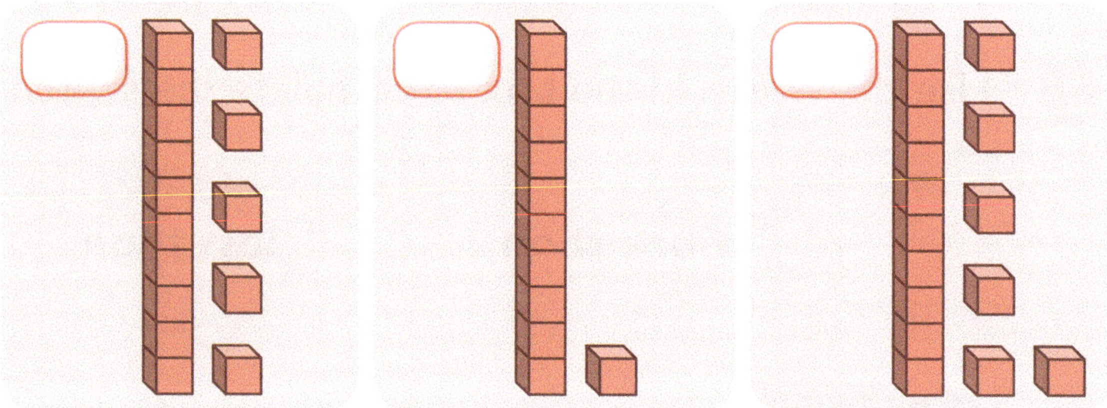

(b)

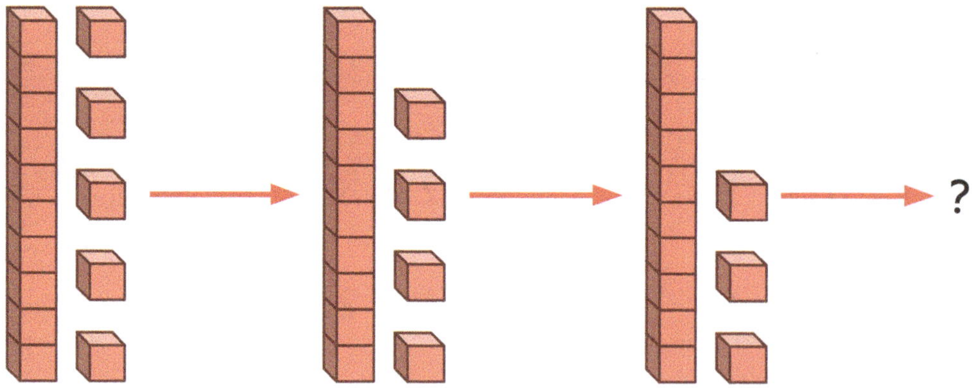

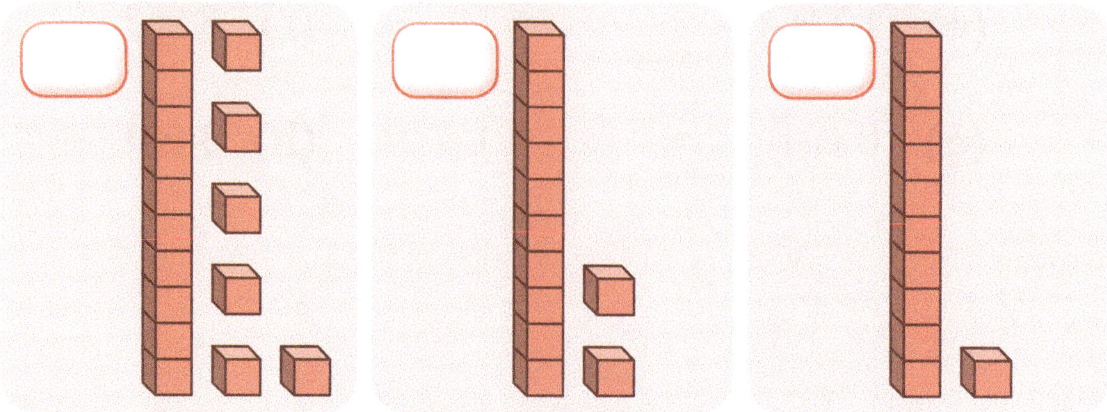

9 Write the number that comes next in the patterns.

(a) 13, 14, 15, ☐

(b) 10, 11, 12, ☐

(c) 15, 16, 17, ☐

(d) 12, 14, 16, ☐

(e) 11, 13, 15, ☐

(f) 14, 16, 18, ☐

10 Write the number that comes next in the patterns.

(a) 18, 17, 16, ☐

(b) 13, 12, 11, ☐

(c) 11, 10, 9, ☐

(d) 19, 17, 15, ☐

(e) 15, 13, 11, ☐

(f) 20, 18, 16, ☐

11 Complete the patterns and answer the questions.

(a) 12 — 13 — 14 — 15

Each number is [1] more / less.

(b) [ ] — 15 — 14 — [ ]

Each number is [ ] more / less.

(c) 13 — [ ] — 17 — [ ]

Each number is [ ] more / less.

(d)

11			17

Each number is ☐ more / less.

(e)

18	16		

Each number is ☐ more / less.

(f)

16		18	

Each number is ☐ more / less.

Practice 7: Ordinal numbers

1 Circle the correct animal.

(a) Which snail is 3rd?

(b) Which spider is 5th?

(c) Which chick is 8th?

(d) Which animal is last?

2 Circle the correct object.

(a) Which bird is fourth?

(b) Which tortoise is 10th?

(c) Which ant is fourth?

(d) Which lizard is seventh?

3 Label their positions.

4 Write the positions of the animals in words.

First

5 Complete the sentences.

(a) The elephant is just behind the ________.

(b) The duck is just in front of the ________.

(c) The ________ is between the cat and the tortoise.

(d) The ________ is last in the race.

6 Match the word to the position.

	fifth	1st
	first	2nd
	fourth	3rd
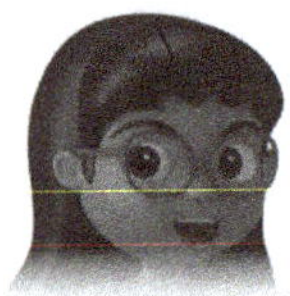	second	4th
	third	5th
	sixth	6th
	ninth	7th
	seventh	8th
	tenth	9th
	eighth	10th

Problem Solving

The Max Maths team had a race.

Use the clues below to fill in the blanks.

Clues:

- Toby finished third. He finished before Padma.
- Tya finished just ahead of Jade.
- Jade was not last.

1. Jade finished [ ].
2. Padma finished [ ].
3. Toby finished [ ].
4. Tya finished [ ].
5. Han finished [ ].

2 Addition to 20

Practice 1: Addition by counting on

1. There are 5 people at the bus stop.

   2 people join them.

   How many people are there altogether?

Count on to show how many people there are altogether.

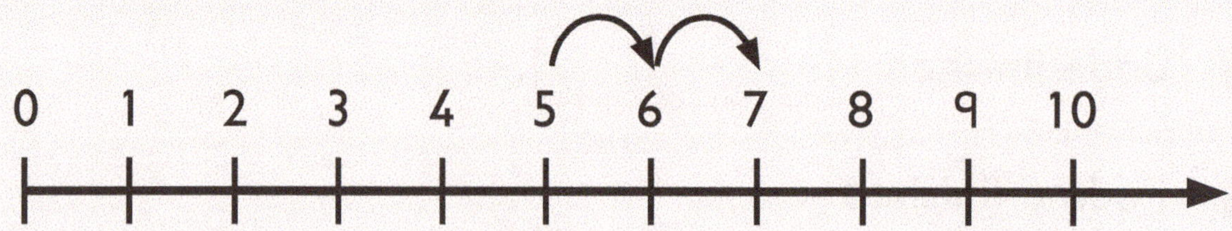

Fill in the blanks.

5 + ☐ = ☐

There are ☐ people altogether.

2 There are some black beads and some red beads.

How many beads are there altogether?

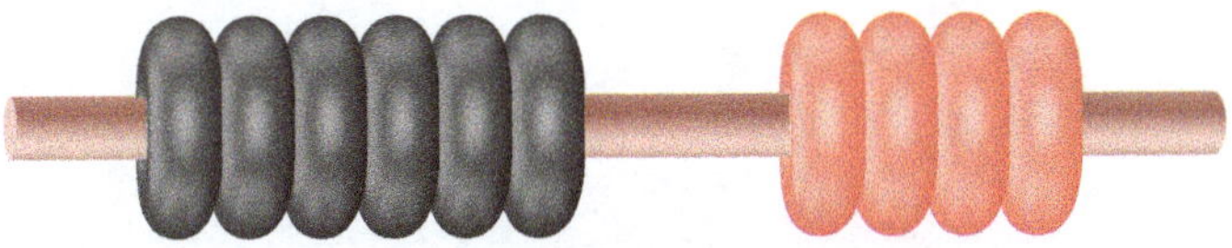

Count on to show how many beads there are altogether.

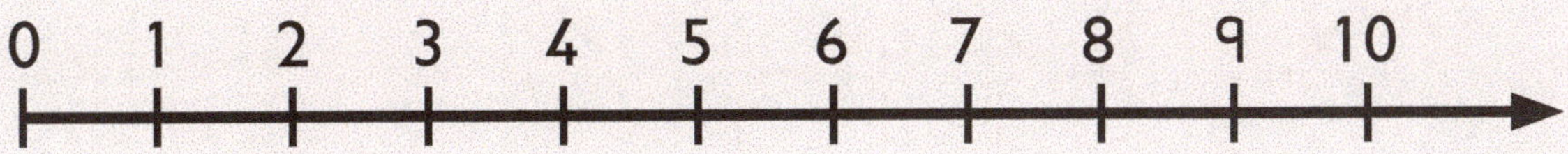

Fill in the blanks.

☐ + ☐ = ☐

There are ☐ beads altogether.

3 Find the answer by counting on.

(a) 6 + 2 = ☐

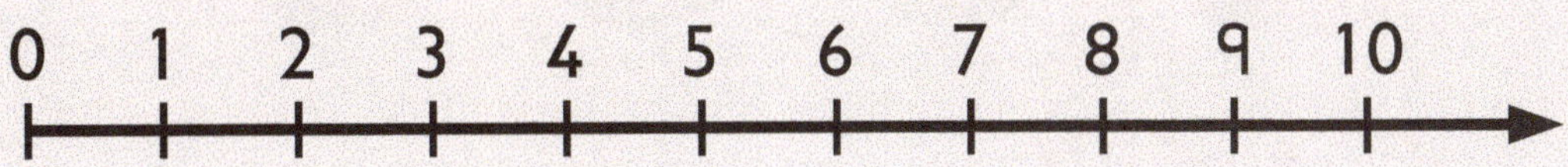

(b) 3 + 6 = ☐

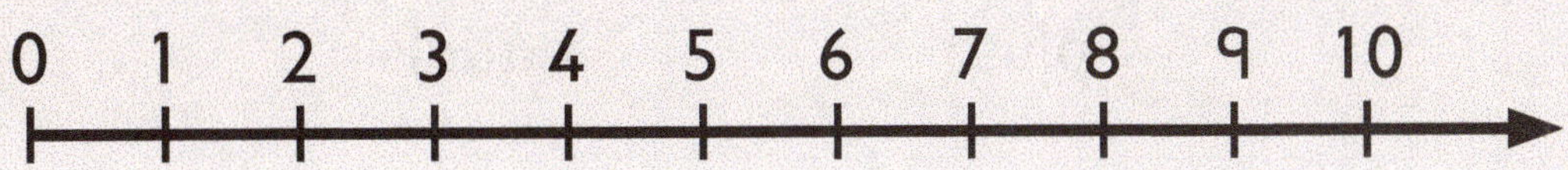

4 Count on from the bigger number.

How many cherries are there altogether?

6 ☐ ☐ ☐

6 + ☐ = ☐ Six plus ☐ equals ☐.

5 Count on from the bigger number.

How many chicken pieces are there altogether?

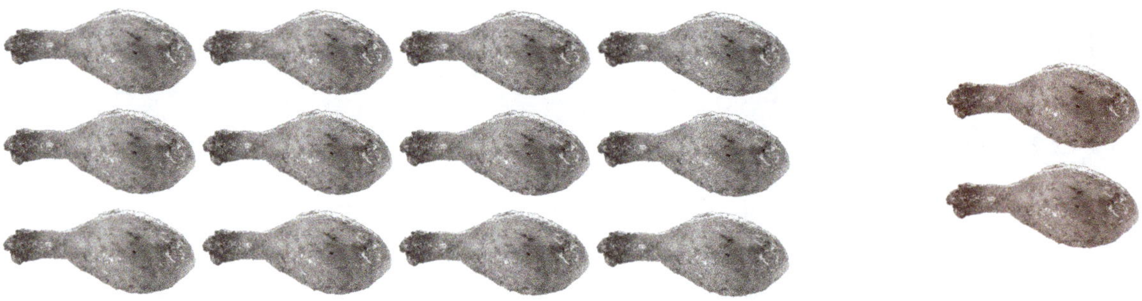

12 ☐ ☐

12 + ☐ = ☐

☐ plus ☐ equals ☐.

6 Fill in the blanks.

(a)

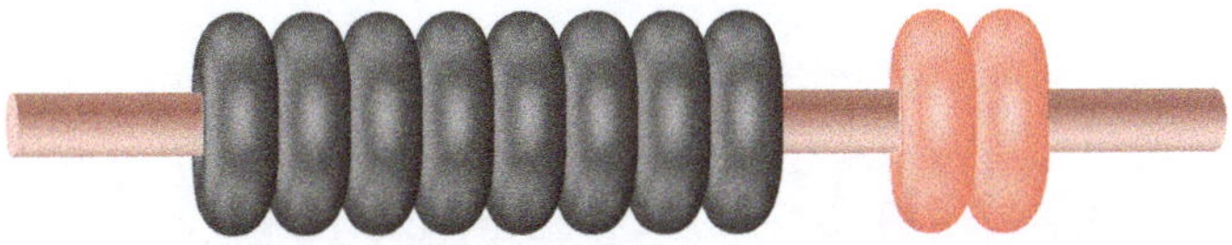

___ + ___ = ___

___ plus ___ equals ___.

(b)

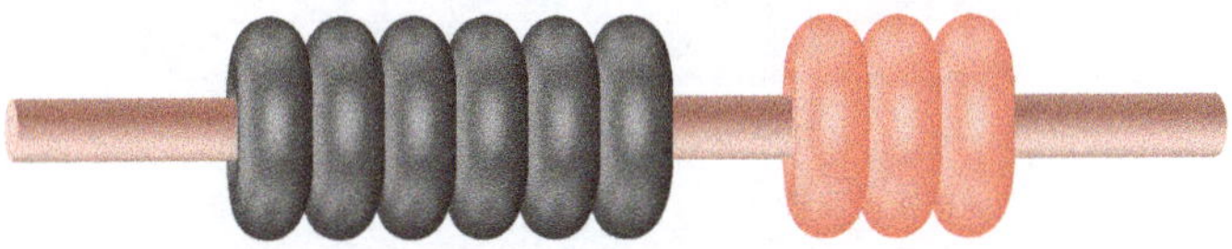

___ + ___ = ___

___ plus ___ equals ___.

(c)

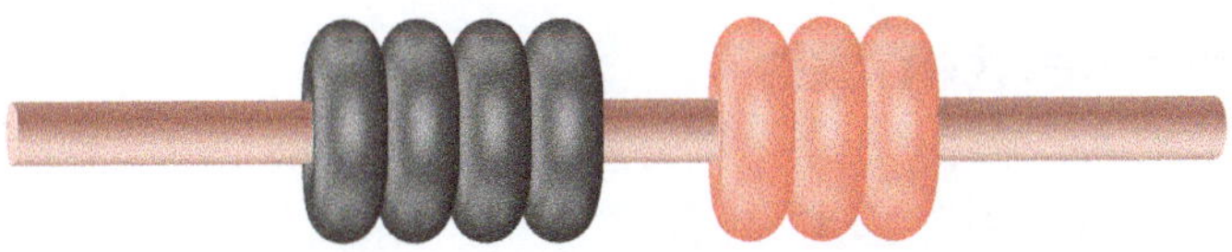

___ + ___ = ___

___ plus ___ equals ___.

7 Circle the picture that matches the addition sentence.

Example

2 + 1 = 3 

(a) 4 + 5 = ☐ 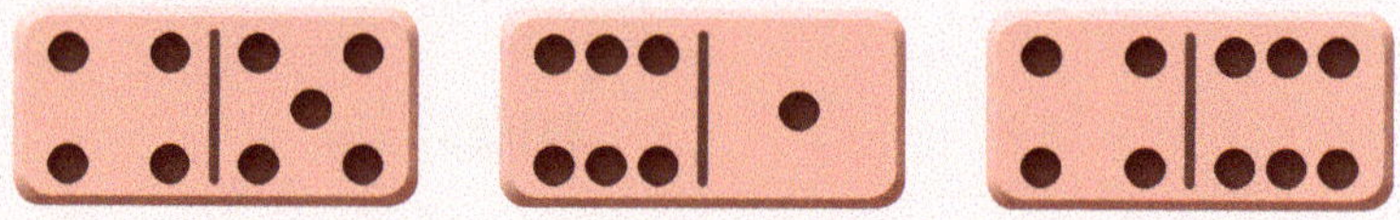

(b) 6 + 1 = ☐ 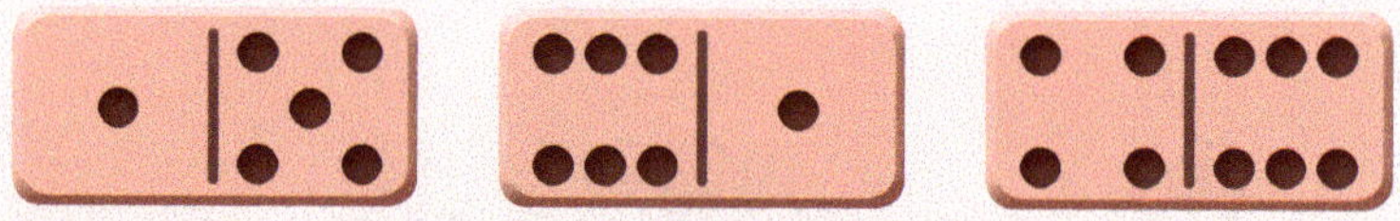

(c) 3 + 0 = ☐ 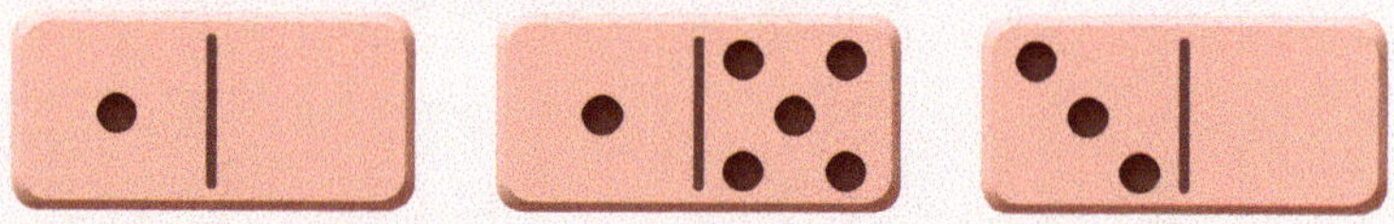

(d) 3 + 3 = ☐ 

8 Match the addition sentences.

two plus four equals six •	• 8 + 1 = 9
four plus three equals seven •	• 6 + 2 = 8
eight plus one equals nine •	• 2 + 4 = 6
five plus zero equals five •	• 4 + 3 = 7
six plus two equals eight •	• 5 + 0 = 5
three plus six equals nine •	• 3 + 6 = 9

Practice 2: Addition using number bonds

1 Complete the number bonds.

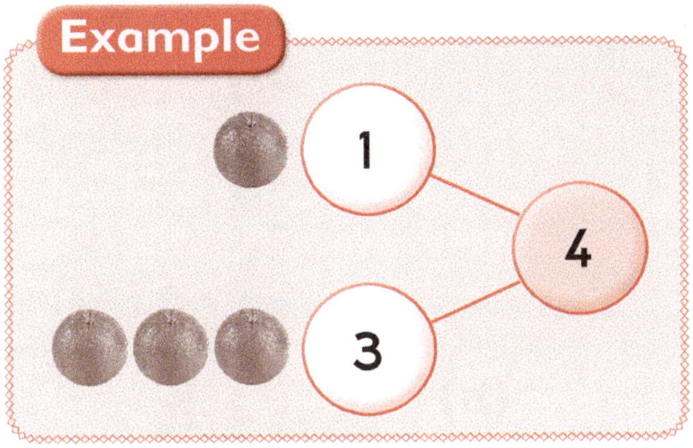

(a)

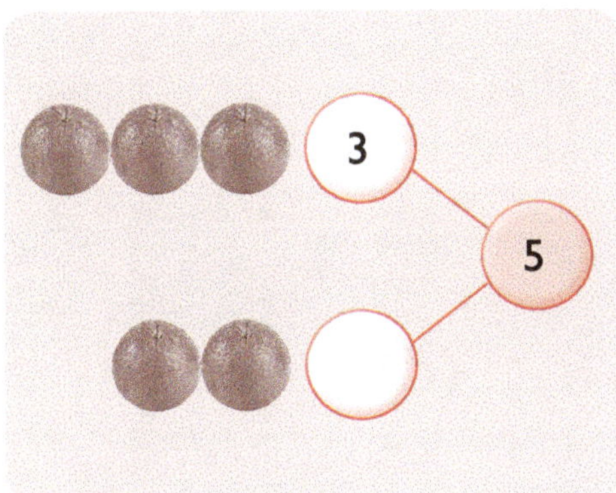

(b)

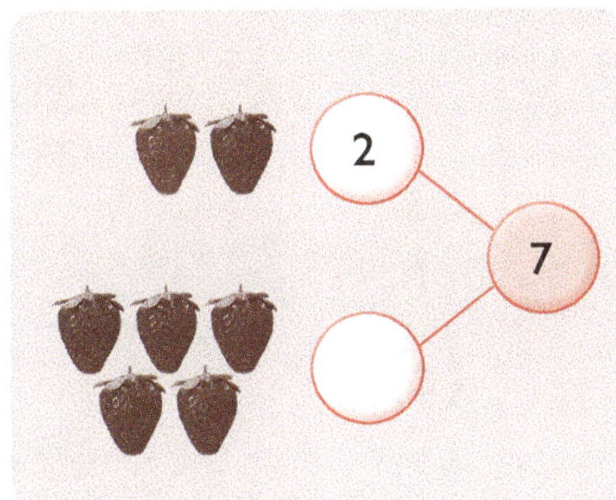

(c)

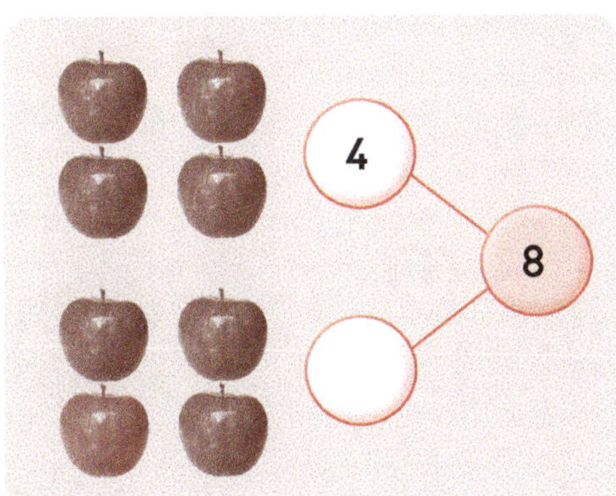

(d)

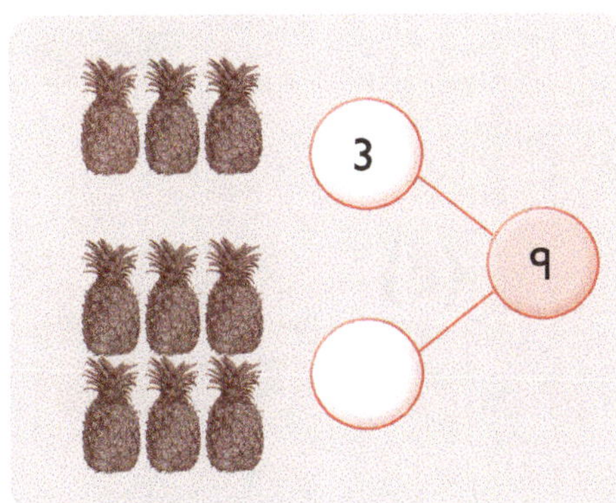

2 Complete the number bonds.

Example

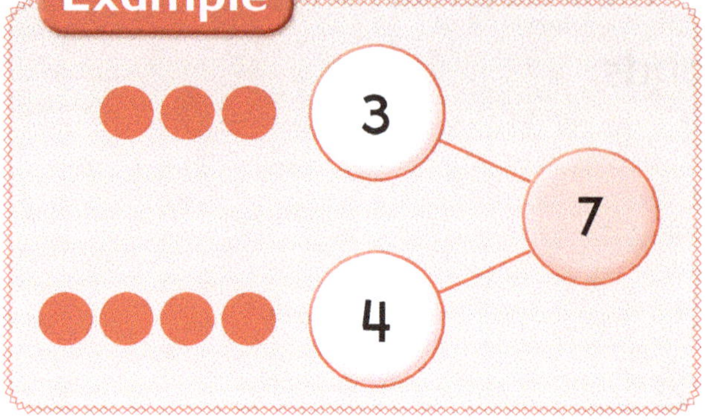

(a)

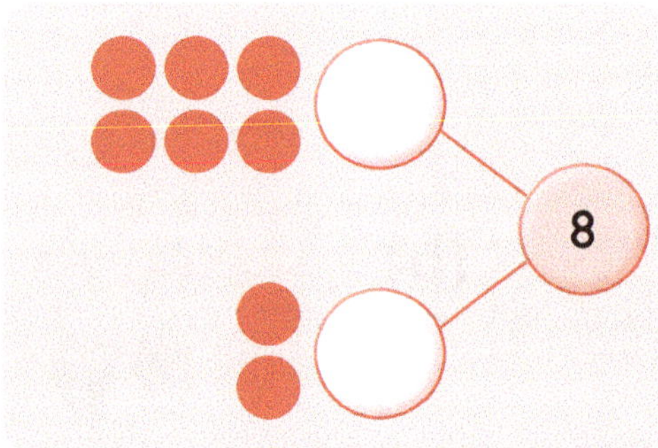

(b)

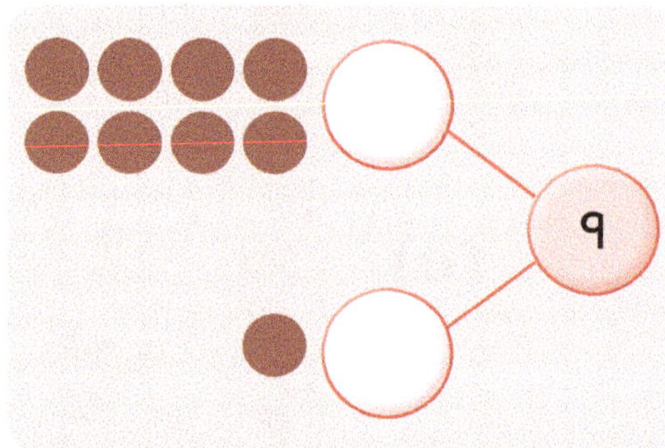

(c)

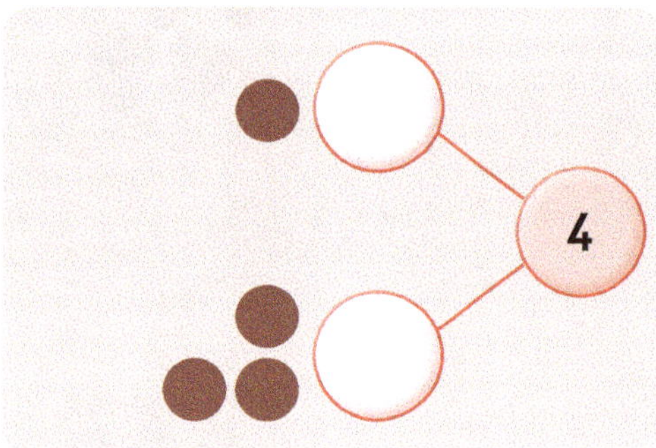

(d)

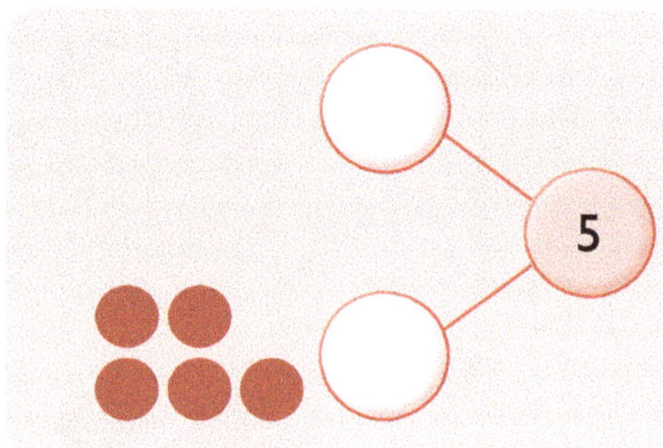

(e)

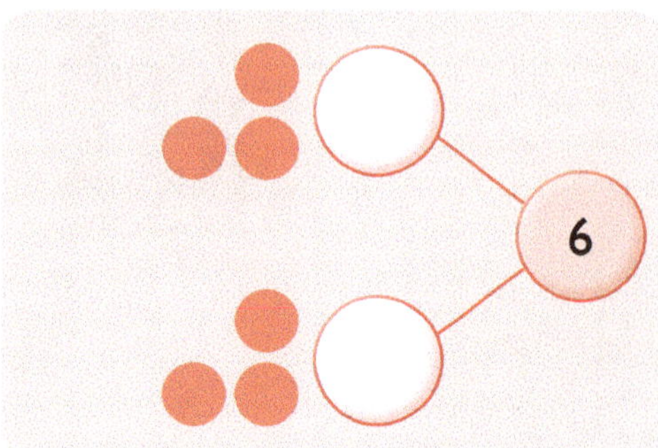

(f)

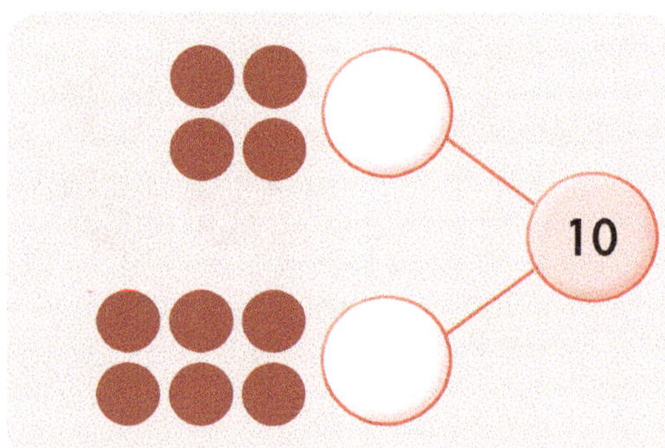

3 Look at the pictures. Make a number bond.

Example

(a)

(b)

(c)

4 Count the beads and make number bonds.
Complete the sentences.

Example

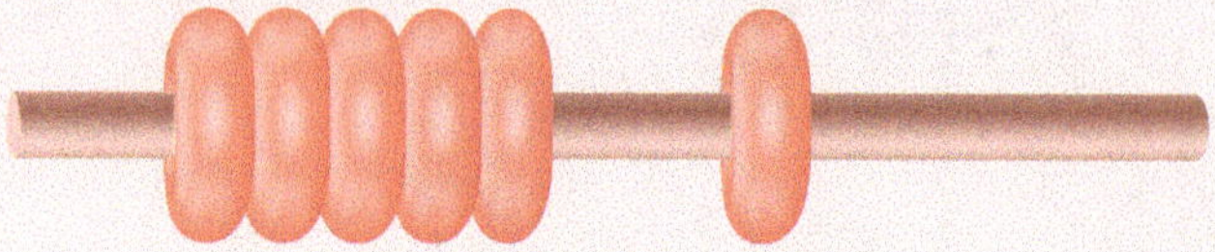

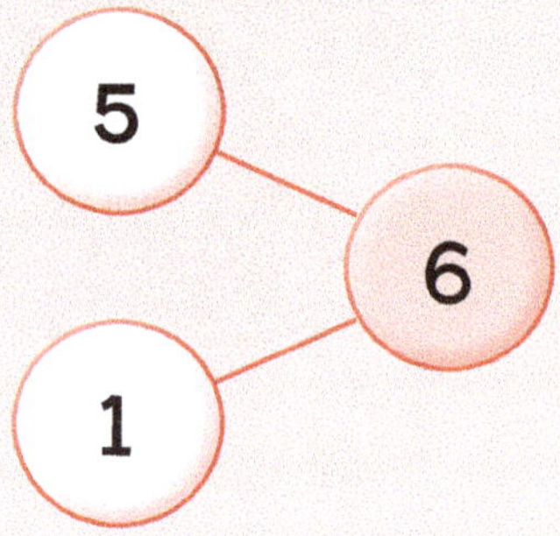

5 and 1 make 6.

(a)

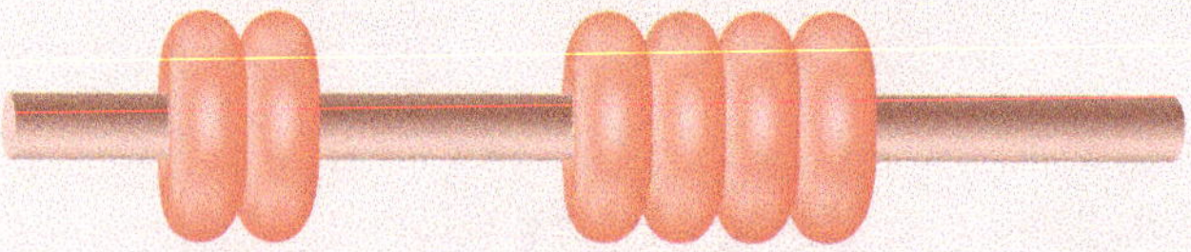

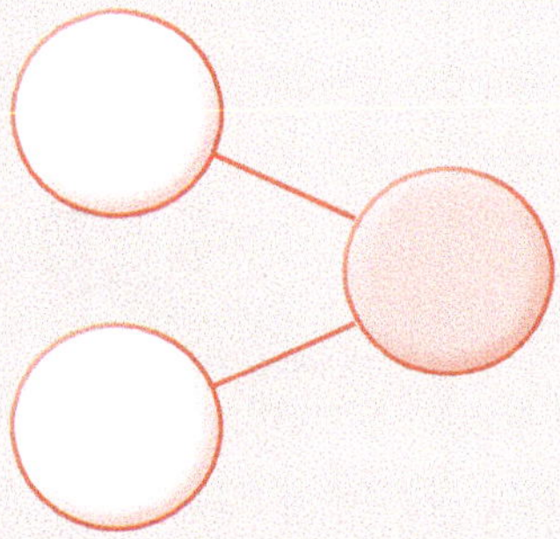

___ and ___ make ___.

(b)

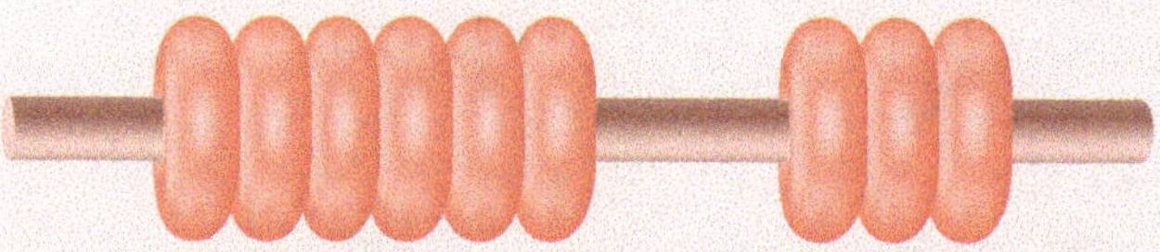

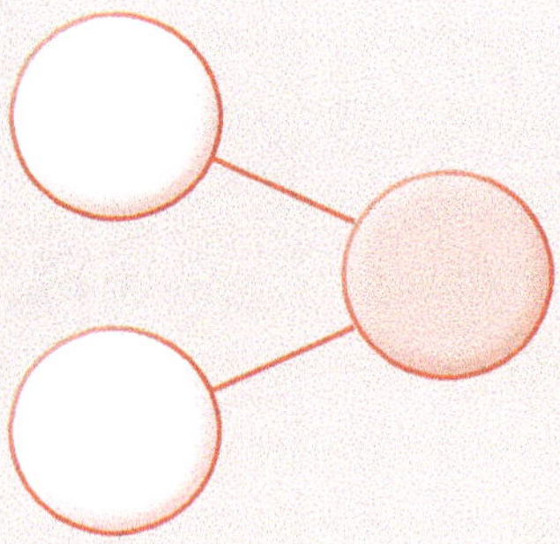

___ and ___ make ___.

(c)

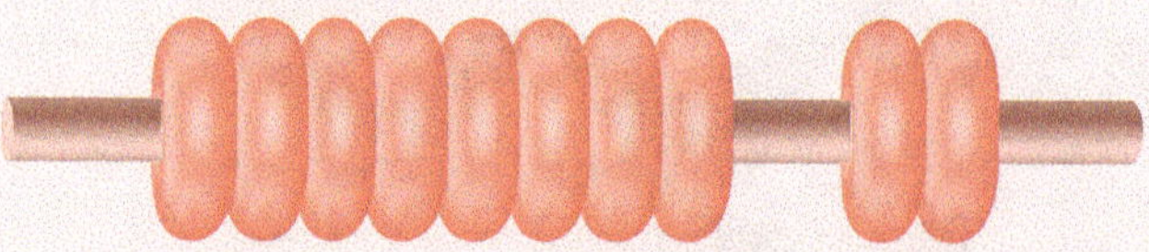

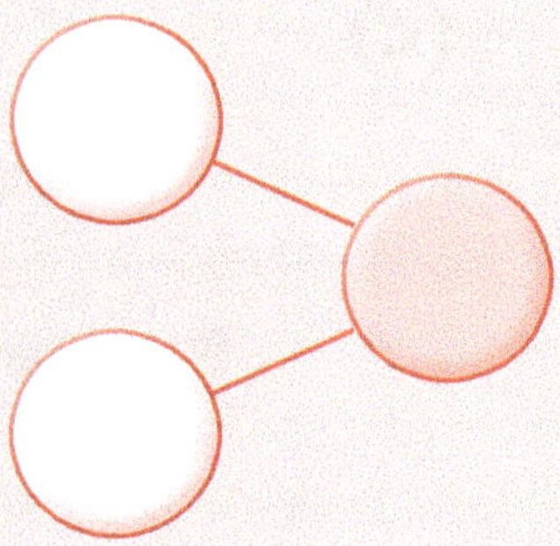

___ and ___ make ___.

5 Make your own number bonds.

Example

Number bond: 4 and 2 make 6

Number bond: 3 and 3 make 6

(a)

Number bond: ___ and ___ make ___

Number bond: ___ and ___ make ___

(b)

Number bond: ___ and ___ make ___

Number bond: ___ and ___ make ___

(c)

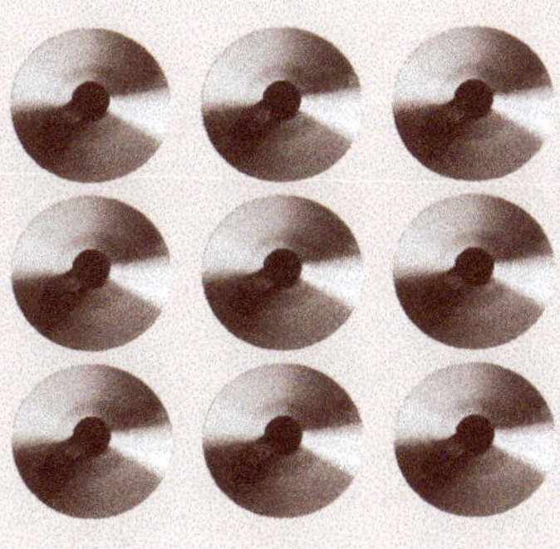

Number bond: ___ and ___ make ___

Number bond: ___ and ___ make ___

6 Make number bonds for the number 10.

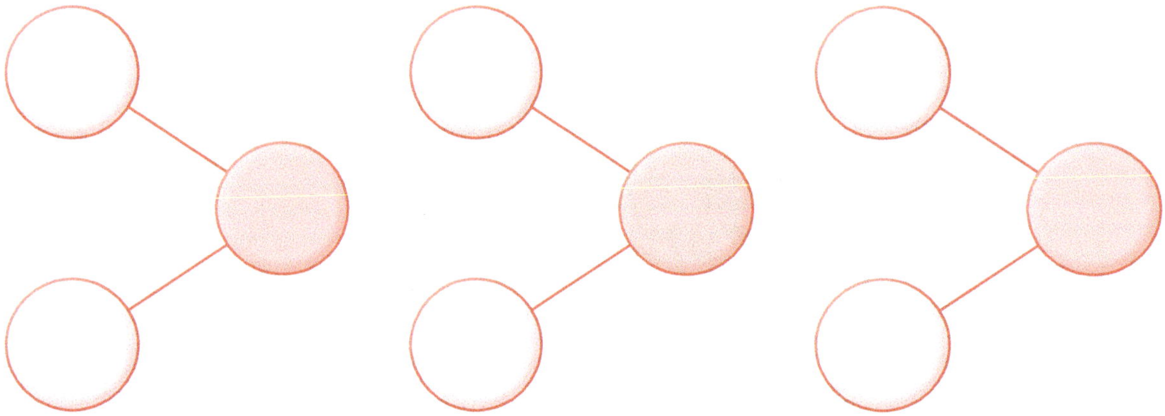

7 Fill in the number bonds for 10 that are not provided above.

Number bonds for 10

☐ and ☐

☐ and ☐

☐ and ☐

8. Tick the numbers that make number bonds of 7.

- [ ] 1 and 5
- [ ] 1 and 6
- [ ] 0 and 8
- [ ] 3 and 4
- [ ] 7 and 0
- [ ] 5 and 3

9. Tick the numbers that make number bonds of 10.

- [ ] one and nine
- [ ] ten and zero
- [ ] three and seven
- [ ] one and eight
- [ ] four and five
- [ ] three and four

10 Colour the boxes to match the addition sentences.

Example

2 + 3 = 5 (2 boxes coloured orange, 3 boxes coloured grey, 5 boxes empty)

(a) 1 + 6 = 7

(b) 6 + 3 = 9

(c) 0 + 4 = 4

(d) 5 + 5 = 10

(e) 8 + 1 = 9

11 Look at the pictures. Write down the addition sentences and complete the number bonds.

(a) How many leaves are there altogether?

[ ] + [ ] = [ ]

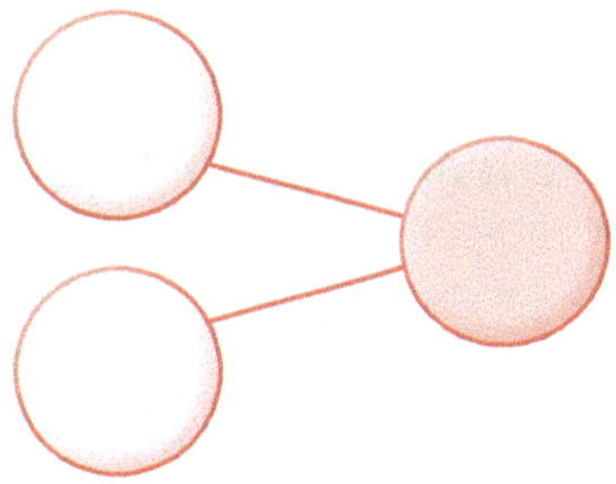

There are [ ] leaves altogether.

(b) How many flowers are there altogether?

[ ] + [ ] = [ ]

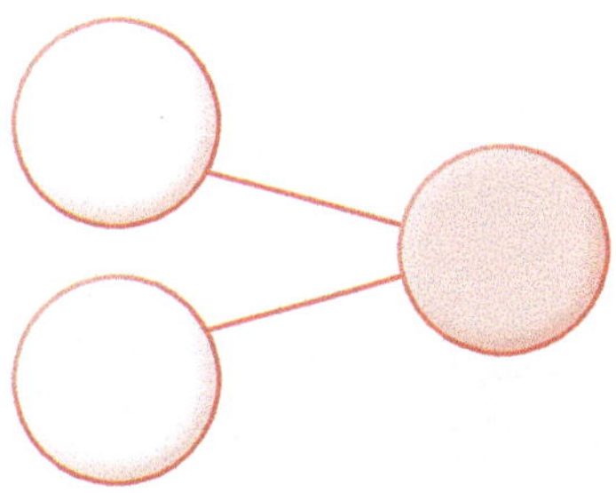

There are [ ] flowers altogether.

(c) How many beads are there altogether?

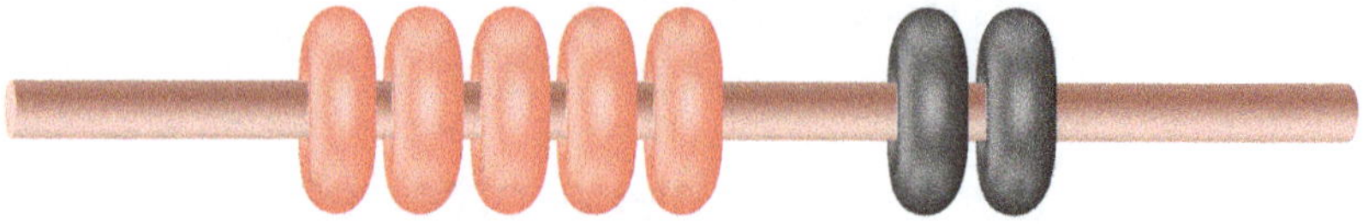

☐ + ☐ = ☐

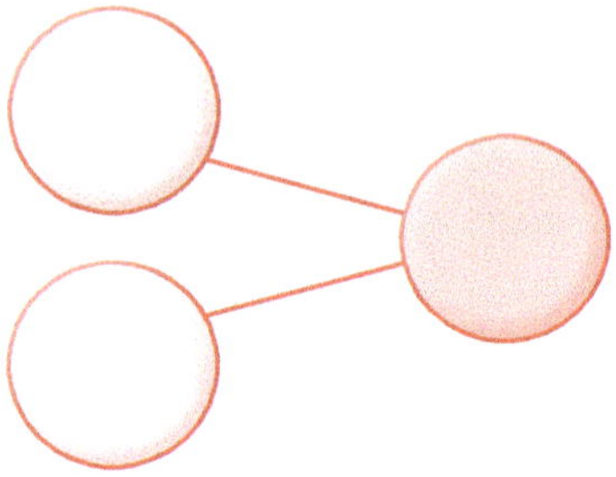

There are ☐ beads altogether.

(d) How many beads are there altogether?

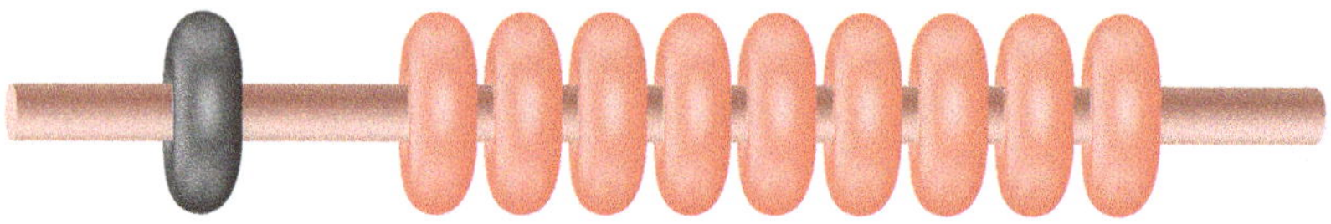

☐ + ☐ = ☐

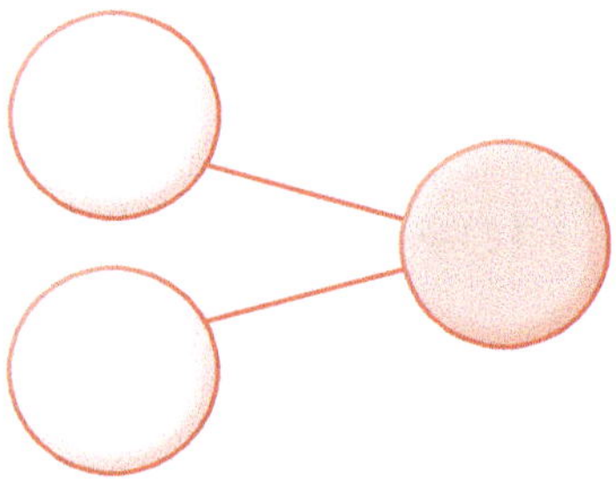

There are ☐ beads altogether.

12 Write down addition sentences and number bonds.

(a) 

___ + ___ = ___

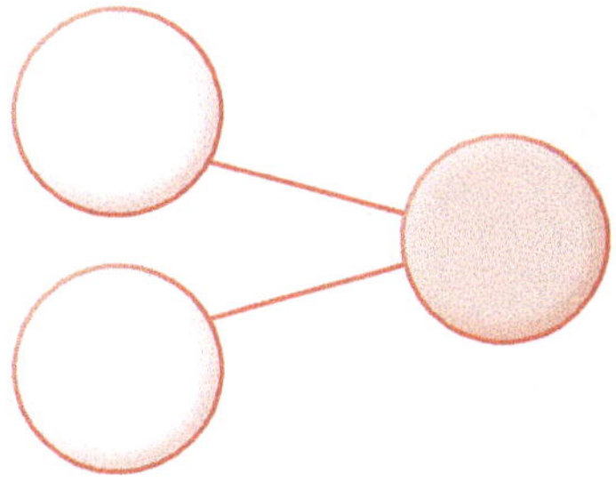

___ and ___ make ___.

(b) 

___ + ___ = ___

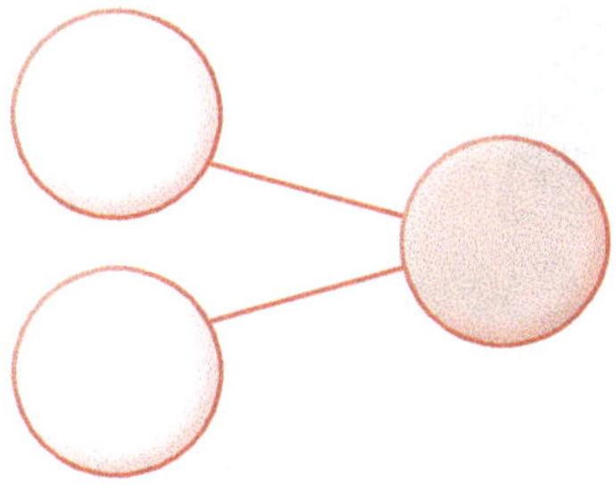

___ and ___ make ___.

(c) 

___ + ___ = ___

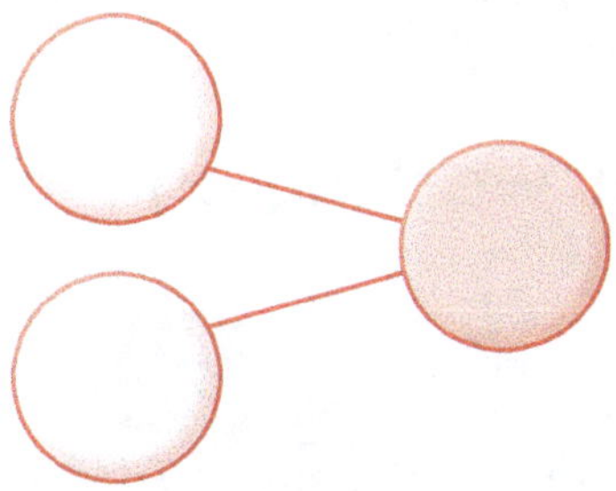

___ and ___ make ___.

Problem Solving

Han has 10 pieces of chocolate.

He wants to give Padma and Tya the same number of pieces.

He wants to give 5 pieces to his family.

He wants to keep 1 piece for himself.

How many pieces will he give to Padma and Tya?

Show your working on a number bond.

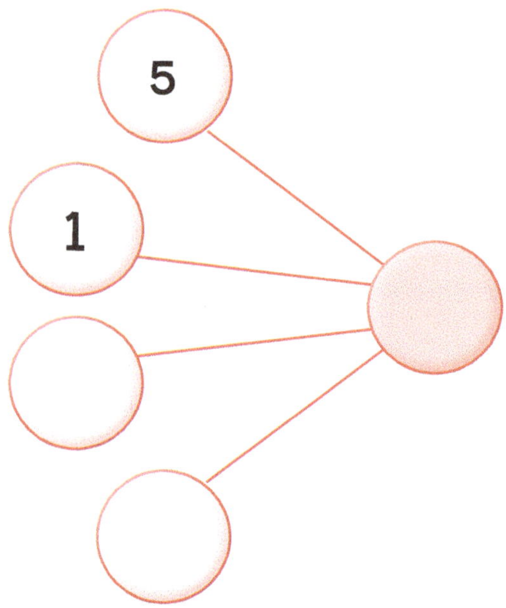

Practice 3: Adding by bridging to 10

1 Count the objects. Write the number and the word.

(a)

11	eleven

(b)

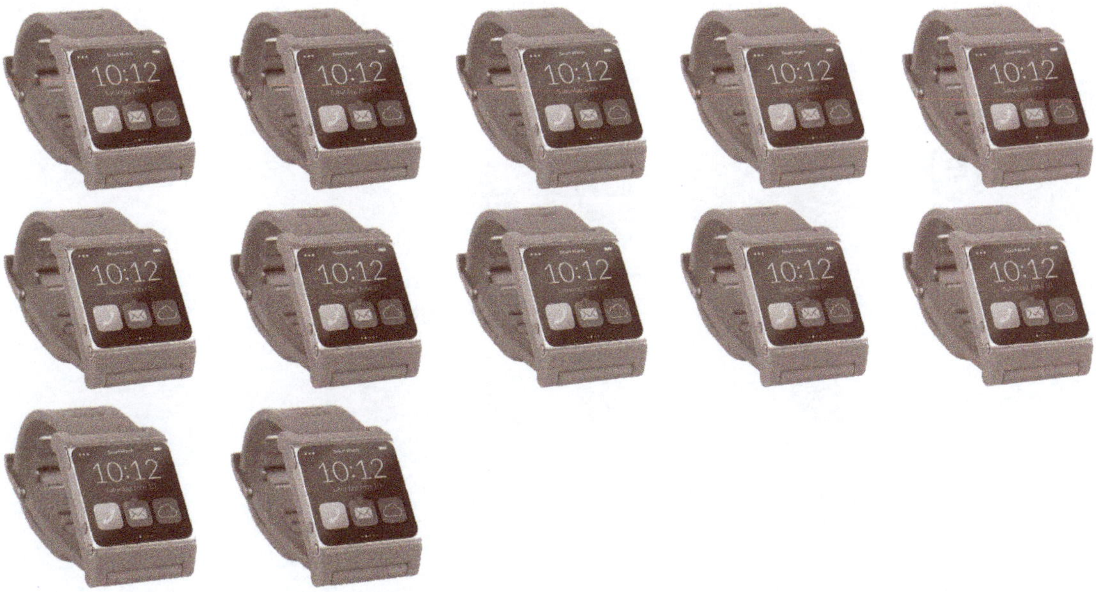

(c)

(d)

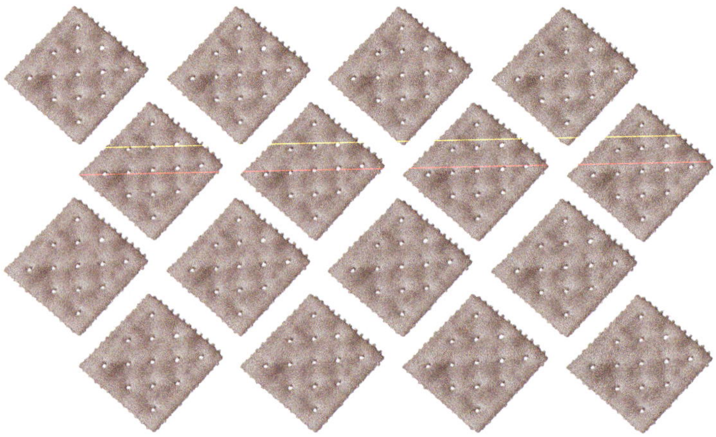

(e)

2 Circle a group of 10. Then add the numbers.

Example

10 + 1 = 11 So, 6 + 5 = 11

(a)

10 + ___ = ___ So, 6 + 6 = ___

(b)

10 + ___ = ___ So, 6 + 9 = ___

(c)

10 + ☐ = ☐ So, 7 + 8 = ☐

(d)

10 + ☐ = ☐ So, 8 + 5 = ☐

3 Colour the white squares to make 10. Then add.

Example

■■■■■■■■ ■■□

8 + 3 = 10 + 1 = 11

(a) □□□□□□□ □□□□□

7 + ☐ = 10 + ☐ = ☐

(b) □□□□□ □□□□□□□□□

5 + ☐ = 10 + ☐ = ☐

(c) □□□□□ □□□□□□□

5 + ☐ = 10 + ☐ = ☐

(d) □□□□□□□□□ □□□□□□

9 + ☐ = 10 + ☐ = ☐

(e) □□□□□□□ □□□□□□□□

7 + ▭ = 10 + ▭ = ▭

(f) □□□□□□ □□□□□□

6 + ▭ = 10 + ▭ = ▭

(g) □□□□□□□□ □□□□□□□□

8 + ▭ = 10 + ▭ = ▭

(h) □□ □□□□□□□□□□□□□□

2 + ▭ = 10 + ▭ = ▭

4 Match the beads that show the same number.

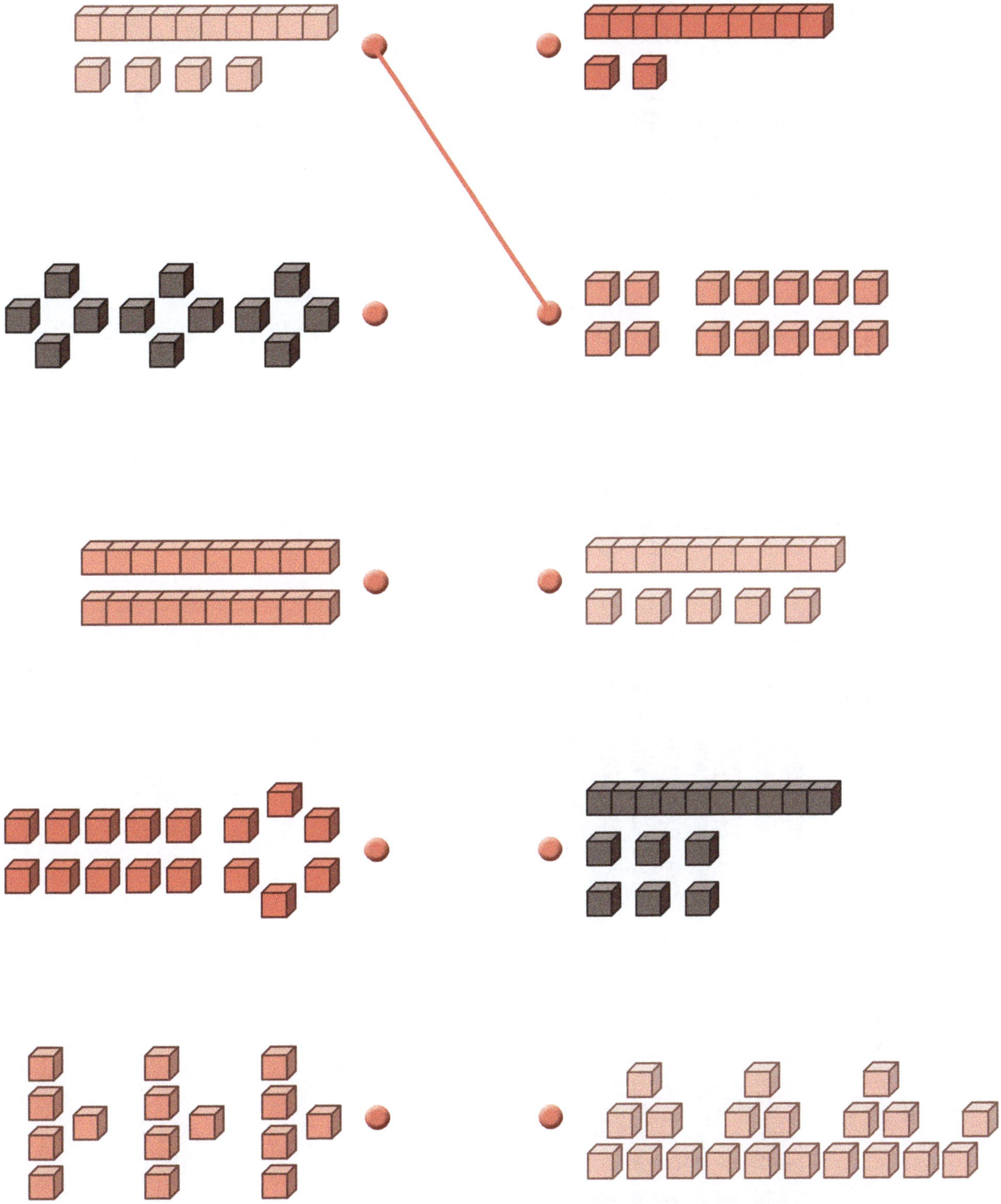

5 Regroup into tens and ones.

Complete the number bonds.

(a) 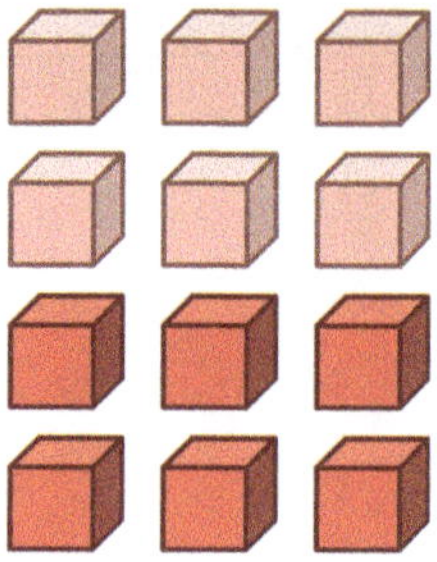 = 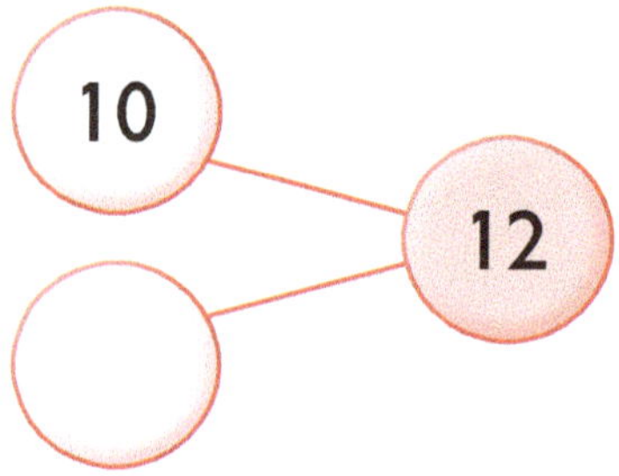

(b) 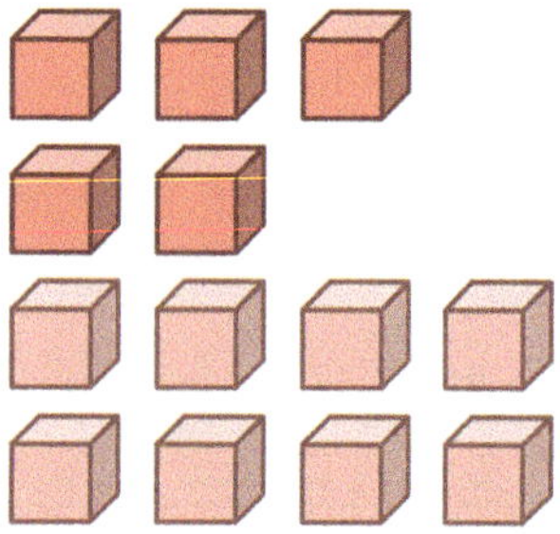 = 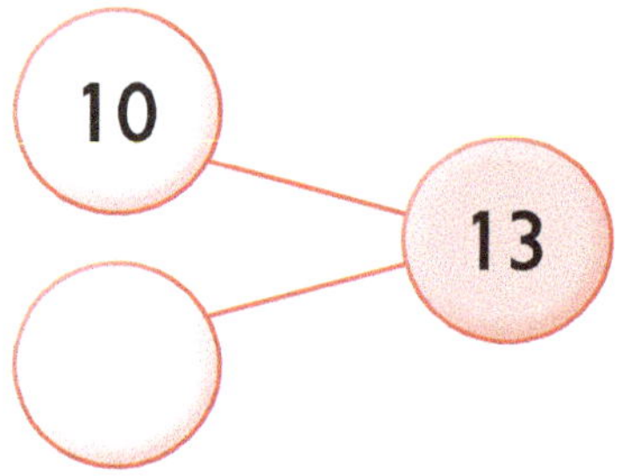

(c) 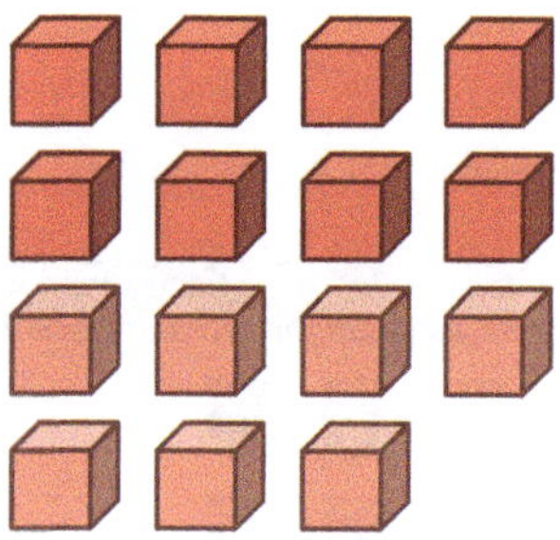 = 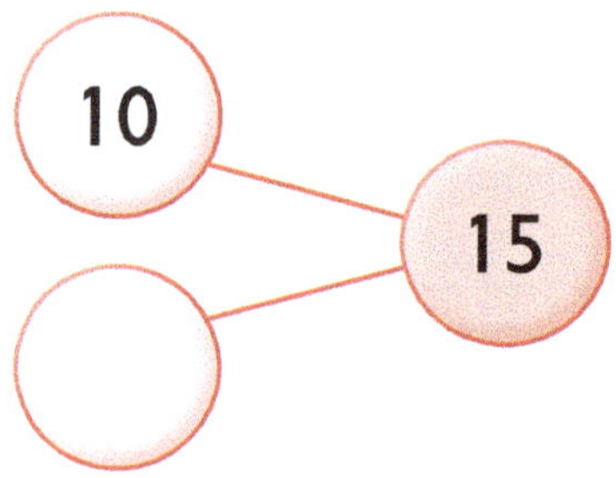

(d)  = 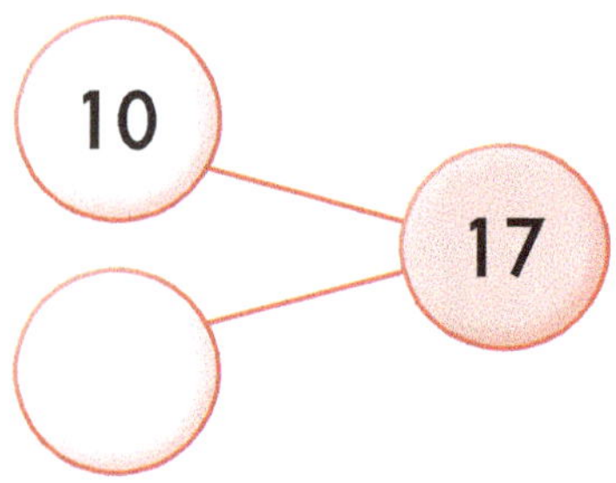

6 Use number bonds to regroup into tens and ones.

Example

8 + 3 = 10 + [1] = [11]

(3 split into 2 and 1)

(a) 4 + 7 = 10 + [ ] = [ ]

(b) 9 + 6 = 10 + [ ] = [ ]

(c) 5 + 7 = 10 + [ ] = [ ]

(d)

$3 + 12 = 10 + \square = \square$

(e)

$4 + 11 = 10 + \square = \square$

(f)

$6 + 12 = 10 + \square = \square$

(g)

$15 + 4 = 10 + \square = \square$

7 Colour the word that completes the number sentence.

(a) 17 + 3 =

twenty eleven thirteen

(b) 7 + 6 =

thirteen sixteen fourteen

(c) 9 + 9 =

eighteen nineteen twenty

8 Fill in the blanks.

(a) 12 + 8 = ☐

(b) 14 + 3 = ☐

(c) 12 + ☐ = 17

(d) ☐ + 2 = 19

(e) 11 + 8 = ☐

(f) 18 + 1 = ☐

(g) 19 + ☐ = 19

(h) ☐ + 4 = 16

9 Toby is trying to regroup  into tens and ones.
Help him by ticking the correct grouping.

(a)

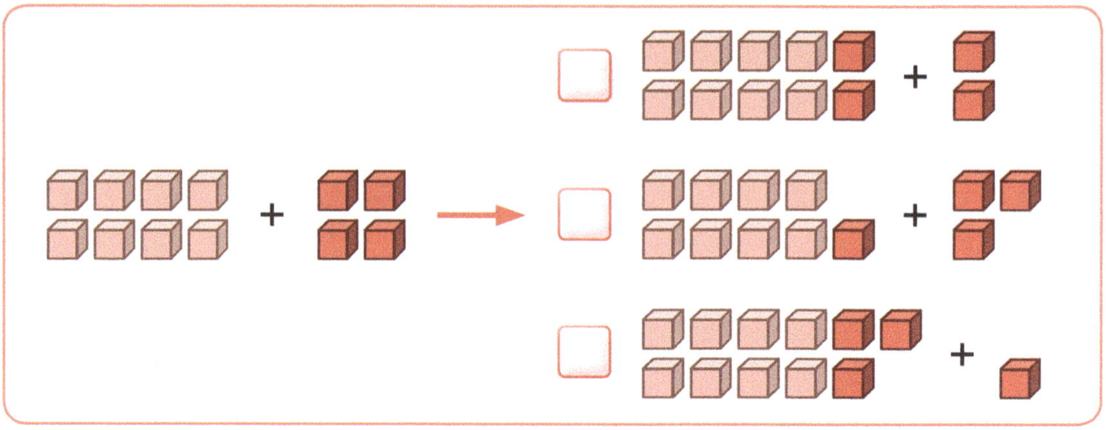

(b)

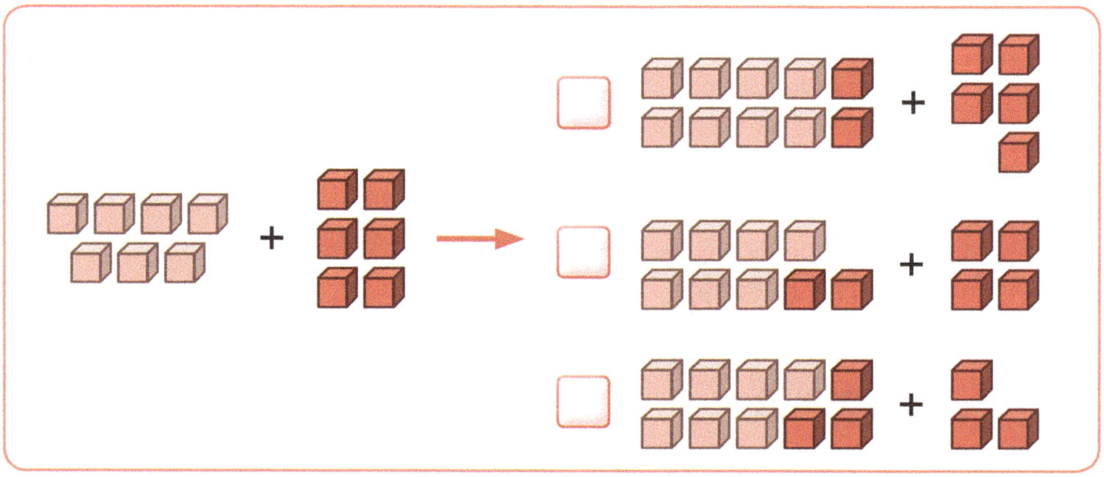

(c)

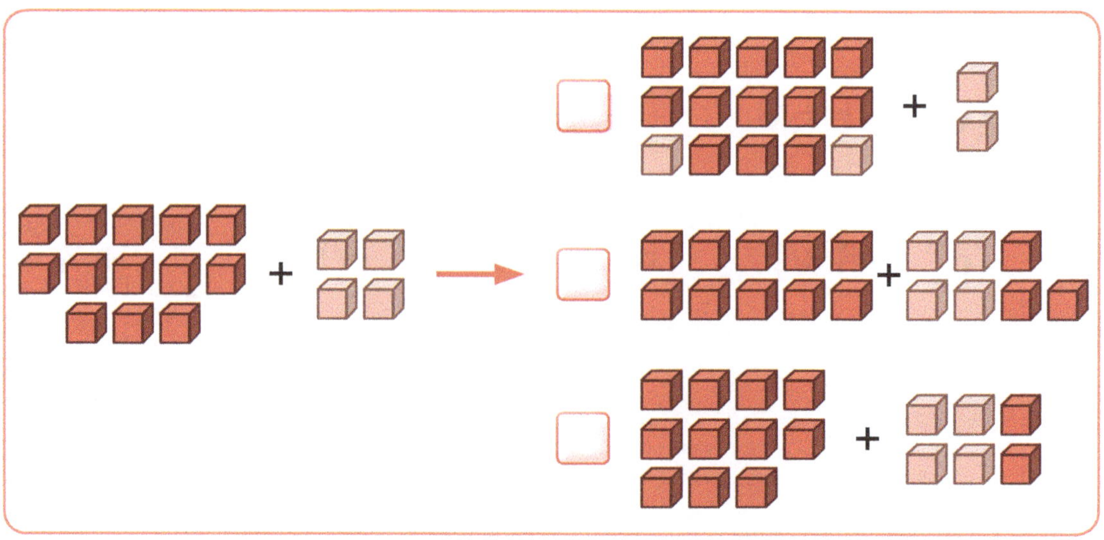

Practice 4: Making and solving addition stories

1 Solve the addition stories.

(a) Samir has 4 bunnies. Jade has 3 teddy bears.

How many soft toys are there altogether?

4 + [ ] = [ ]

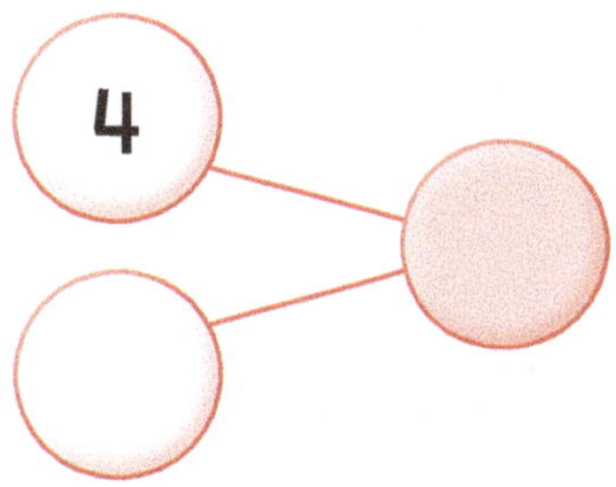

There are [7] soft toys altogether.

(b) There are 5 red balloons. There is 1 white balloon.

How many balloons are there altogether?

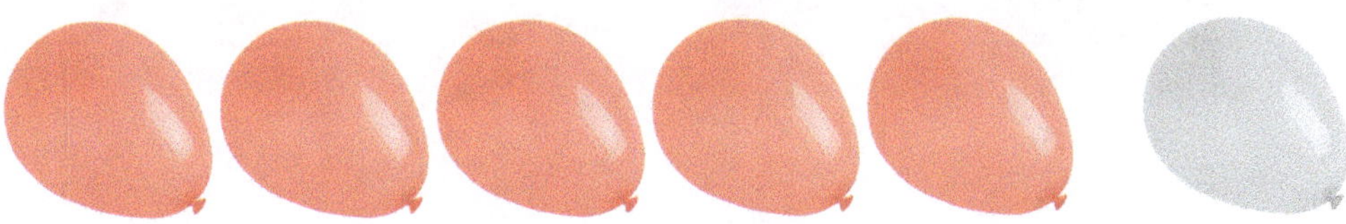

[ ] [ ] [ ] = [ ]

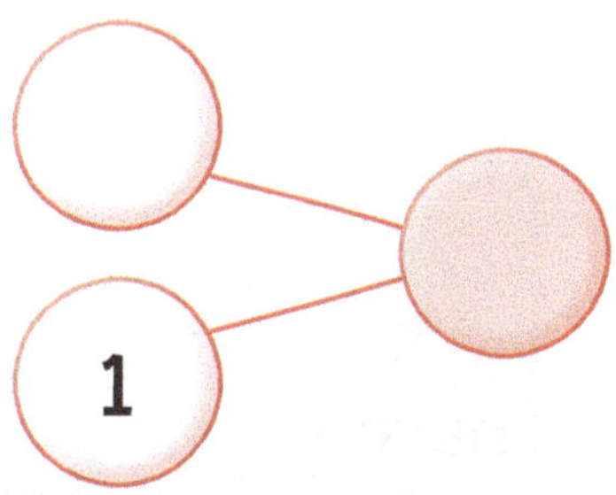

There are [ ] balloons altogether.

(c) There are 7 guinea pigs. There are 6 cats.

How many pets are there altogether?

☐ ☐ ☐ = ☐

There are ☐ pets altogether.

(d) There are 4 circles. There are 8 triangles.

How many shapes are there altogether?

☐ ☐ ☐ = ☐

There are ☐ shapes altogether.

2 Make addition stories and addition sentences.

(a) There are ☐ boys.

There are ☐ girls.

☐ ☐ ☐ ☐ ☐

There are ☐ children altogether.

(b) There are ☐ bananas.

There are ☐ pineapples.

☐ ☐ ☐ ☐ ☐

There are ☐ fruits altogether.

(c) There are ☐ lollipops.

There are ☐ candies.

☐ ☐ ☐ ☐ ☐

There are ☐ sweets altogether.

(d) ☐ faces are happy.

☐ faces are sad.

☐ ☐ ☐ ☐ ☐

There are ☐ faces altogether.

3 Look at the picture. Complete the addition stories.

(a) There are ☐ small bears.

There are ☐ big bears.

There are ☐ teddy bears altogether.

☐ ☐ ☐ ☐ ☐

(b) There are ☐ trucks.

There are ☐ cars.

There are ☐ vehicles altogether.

☐ ☐ ☐ ☐ ☐

(c) There are ☐ big balls.

There are ☐ small balls.

There are ☐ balls altogether.

☐ ☐ ☐ ☐ ☐

4 Look at the picture. Use the words in the word box to help you make and solve your own addition story.

bananas	strawberries	has
buys	altogether	

5. Make your own addition story with the addition sentence.

7 + 8 = 15

____

____

____

____

6. Complete the addition sentences.

(a) 1 + ☐ = 4

(b) ☐ + 3 = 6

(c) ☐ + 4 = 13

(d) 6 + 9 = ☐

(e) 0 + 7 = ☐

(f) 2 + ☐ = 10

(g) 7 + ☐ = 16

(h) 5 + 6 = ☐

(i) ☐ + 5 = 8

(j) 9 + ☐ = 9

(k) 8 + 7 = ☐

(l) 7 + ☐ = 13

Practice 5: Counting by twos, fives and tens

1 Count in twos. Fill in the missing number in the pattern.

(a)

(b)

(c)

2 Count in fives or tens. Fill in the missing numbers in the pattern.

(a)

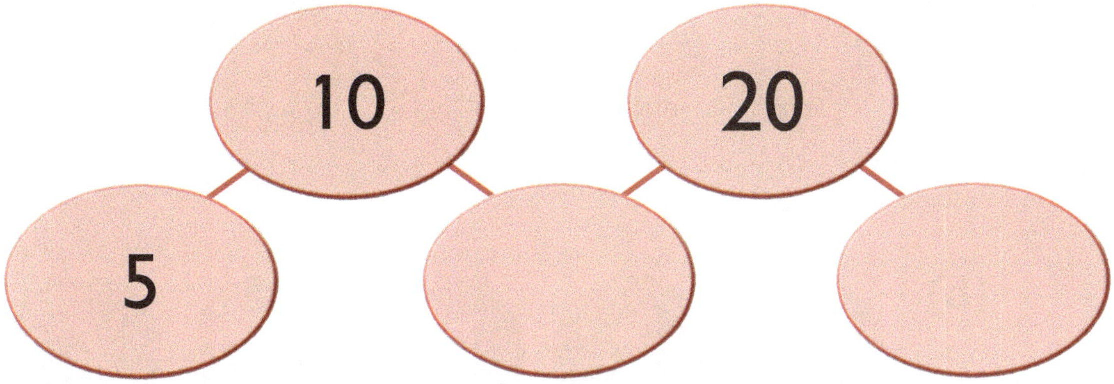

(b)

(c)

(d)

3 Complete the patterns.

(a) 6, 7, ☐, 9, ☐

(b) ☐, 1, 2, ☐, 4

(c) 6, 8, ☐, 12, ☐

(d) 8, ☐, 4, 2, ☐

(e) 50, 60, ☐, 80, ☐

(f) 15, 20, ☐, 30, ☐

Practice 6: Estimating numbers to 30

1 Complete the following.

(a) Estimate the number of ants below.

Estimate: ☐

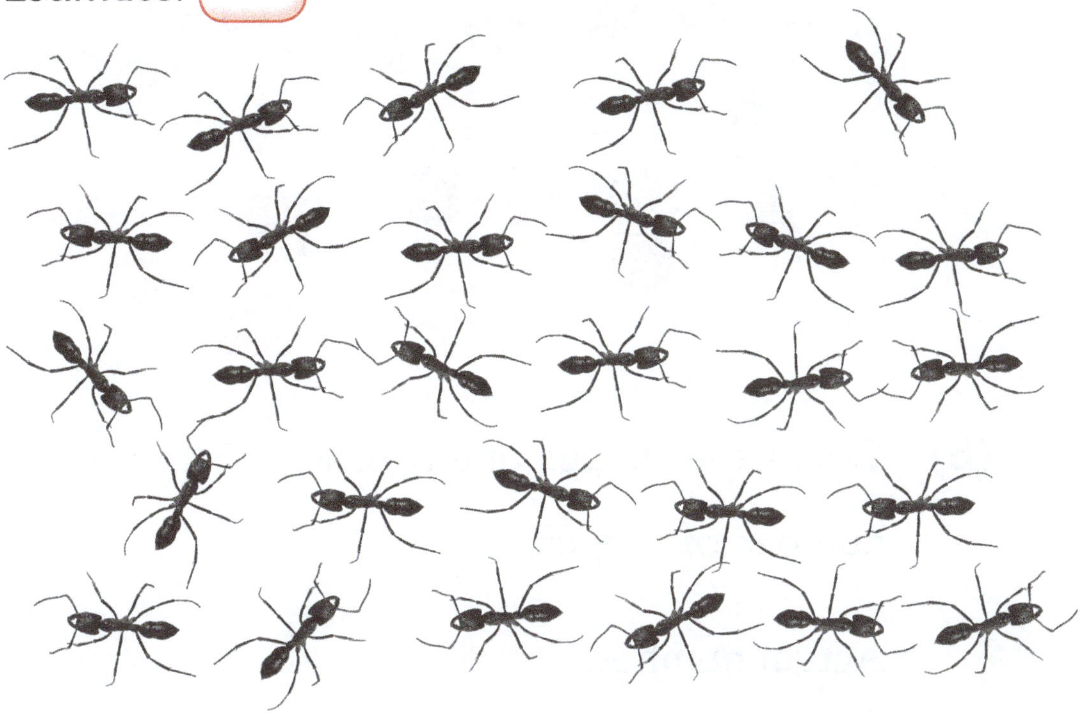

(b) Count the ants one by one. Write down the actual number of ants.

Actual number: ☐

(c) Was your estimate close to the actual number of ants?

☐

2 Complete the following questions.

(a) Estimate the number of shapes below.

Estimate:

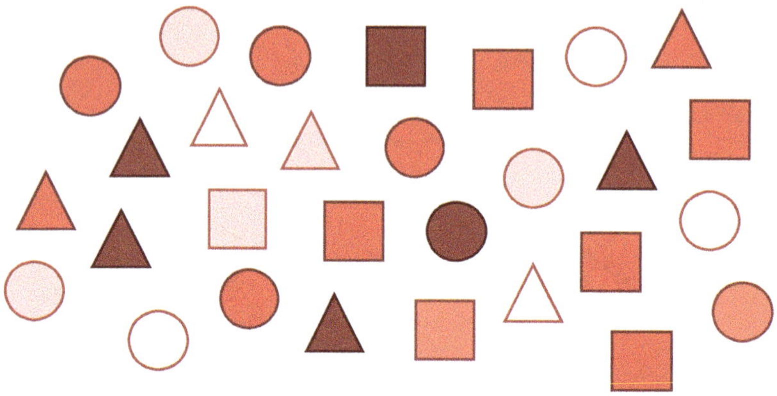

(b) Count the shapes one by one. Write down the actual number of shapes.

Actual number:

(c) Was your estimation close to the actual number of shapes?

(d) Describe how you did your estimate.

Practice 7: Doubling and halving numbers

Write the number sentences for these doubles.

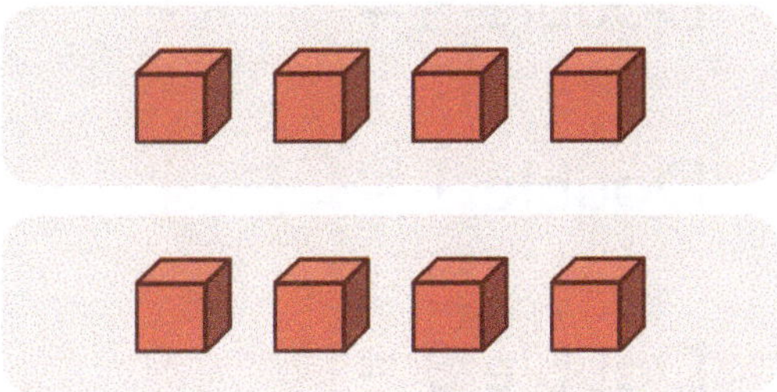

4 + 4 = 8

1 

5 + ☐ = ☐

2 

☐ + ☐ = ☐

3 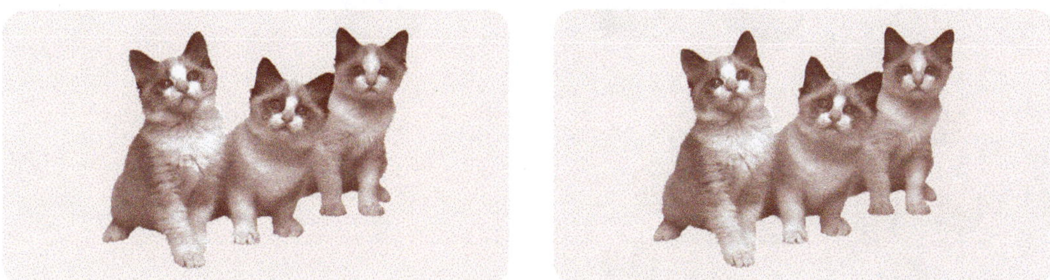

☐ + ☐ = ☐

4 Double these single-digit numbers.

(a) Double 4 = ☐ (b) Double 7 = ☐

(c) Double 2 = ☐ (d) Double 9 = ☐

(e) Double 6 = ☐ (f) Double 1 = ☐

(g) Double 3 = ☐ (h) Double 8 = ☐

5 Draw a circle around the objects to show half of each set.

(a)

(b)

(c)

(d)

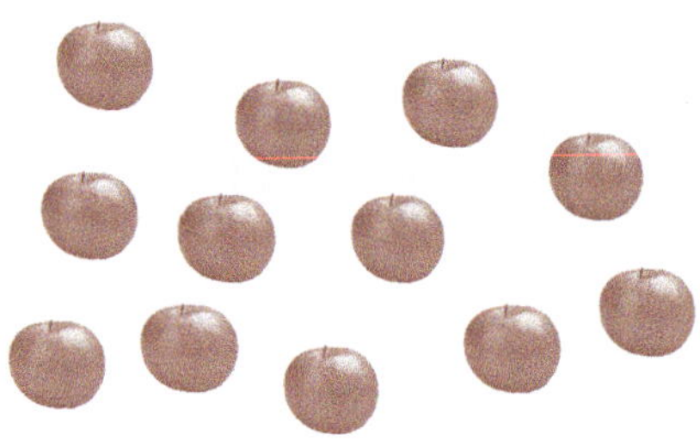

(e)

6 Circle the word that makes the sentences correct.

(a) Numbers that can be shared evenly into two sets are even / odd.

(b) Odd / even numbers cannot be halved equally.

(c) Odd / even numbers always have one left over when they are being shared between two.

7 Halve these numbers.

(a) Half of 10 = ☐

(b) Half of 4 = ☐

(c) Half of 6 = ☐

(d) Half of 12 = ☐

(e) Half of 14 = ☐

(f) Half of 8 = ☐

(g) Half of 2 = ☐

(h) Half of 20 = ☐

(i) Half of 16 = ☐

(j) Half of 18 = ☐

Practice 8: Doubling near numbers

1 Circle all the ways you could find the solution.

(a) How many cubes are there altogether?

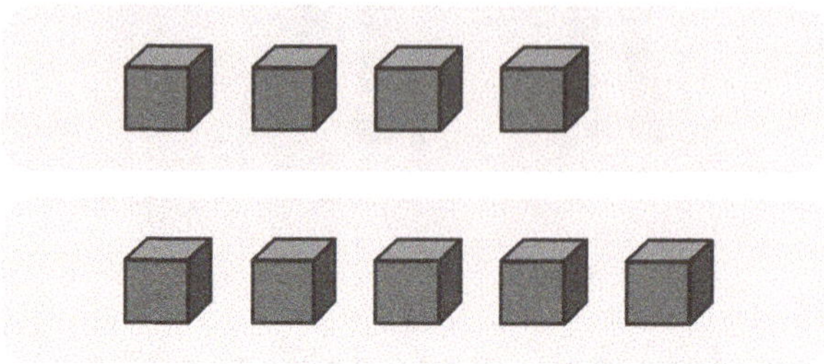

Double 4 then take away 1 Double 5 then take away 1

Double 4 then add 1 Double 5 then add 1

(b) How many seagulls are there altogether?

Double 3 then take away 1 Double 2 then take away 1

Double 3 then add 1 Double 2 then add 1

(c) How many balls are there altogether?

Double 6 then take away 1

Double 6 then add 1

Double 5 then take away 1

Double 5 then add 1

(d) How many cats are there altogether?

Double 2 then take away 1

Double 3 then take away 1

Double 2 then add 1

Double 3 then add 1

3 Subtraction within 20

Practice 1: Subtraction by taking away

1. There are 5 frogs.

   2 frogs hop away.

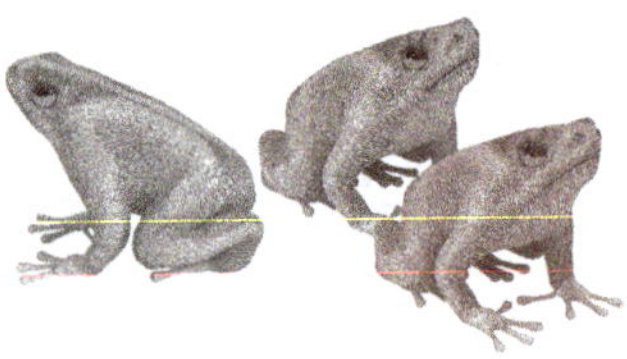

   5 − ___ = ___

   There are ___ frogs left.

2. There are 5 pigeons.

   4 pigeons fly away.

   ___ − ___ = ___

   There is ___ pigeon left.

3 Complete the subtraction sentence.

Cross out the objects to help you.

(a) $7 - 2 = \square$

(b) $8 - 4 = \square$

(c) $10 - 3 = \square$

4 Look at the beads.

Write the subtraction sentence.

Example

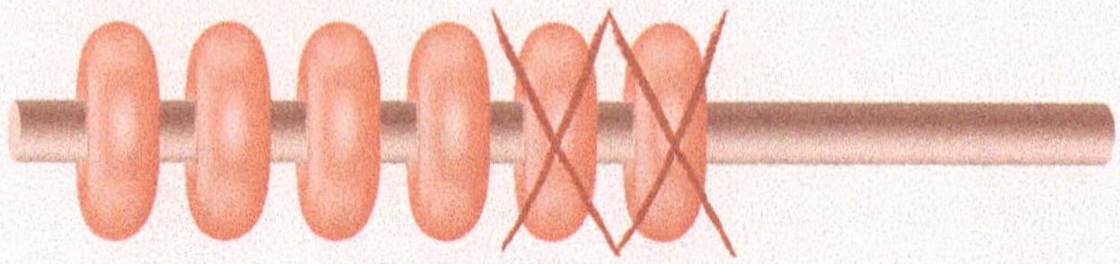

6 − 2 = 4

(a)

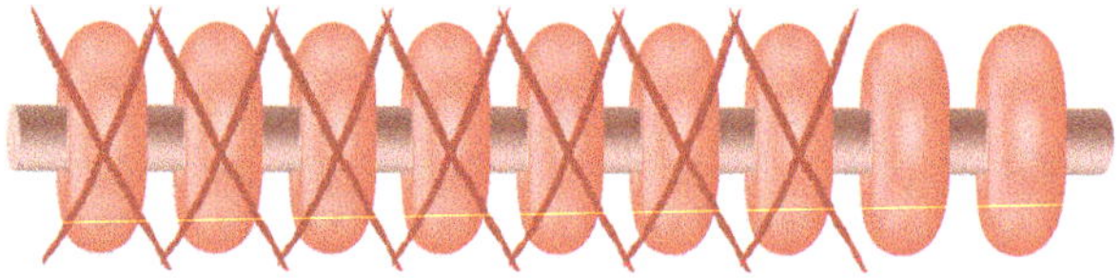

☐ − ☐ = ☐

(b)

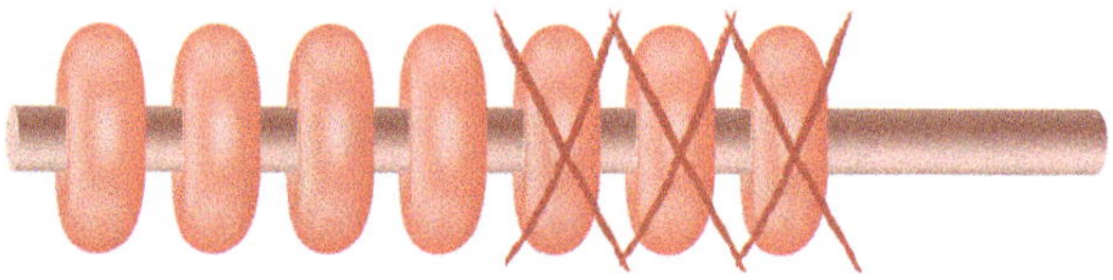

☐ − ☐ = ☐

(c)

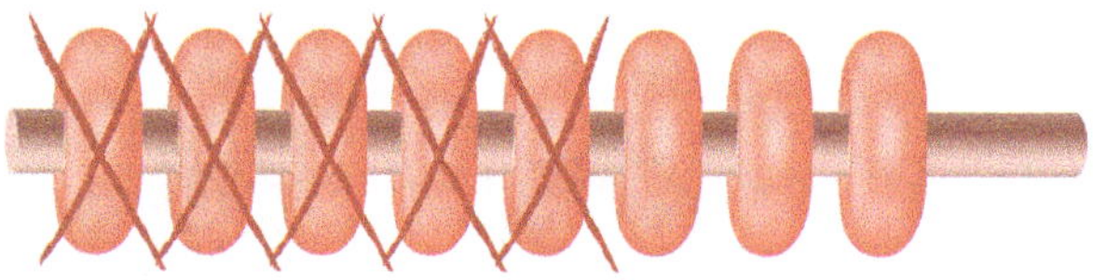

☐ − ☐ = ☐

(d)

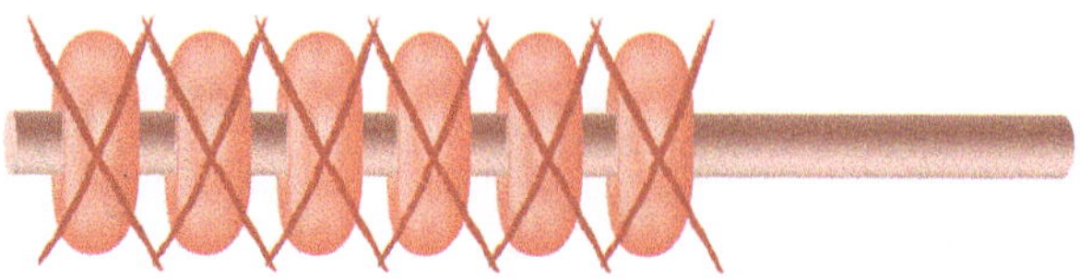

☐ − ☐ = ☐

5 Match the subtraction sentence to the picture and fill in the blanks.

10 − 7 = ☐

8 − 6 = ☐

9 − 8 = ☐

5 − 5 = ☐

10 − 6 = ☐

7 − 5 = ☐

10 − 3 = ☐

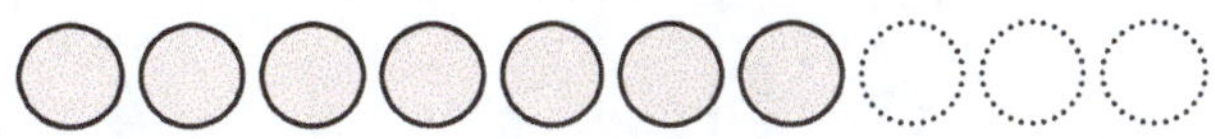

Practice 2: Subtraction by counting back

1 There are 8 keys.

1 key is taken away.

Count back from 8 to show how many keys are left.

$\square - \square = \square$

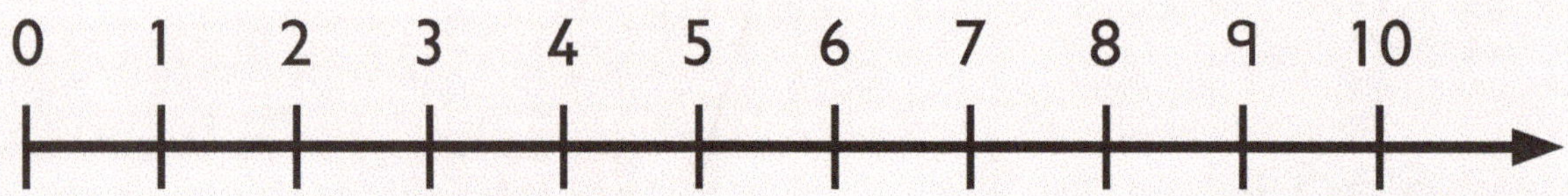

2 There are 8 eggs in a carton.

3 eggs are taken out of the carton.

How many eggs are left in the carton? Use the number line to count back.

$\square - \square = \square$

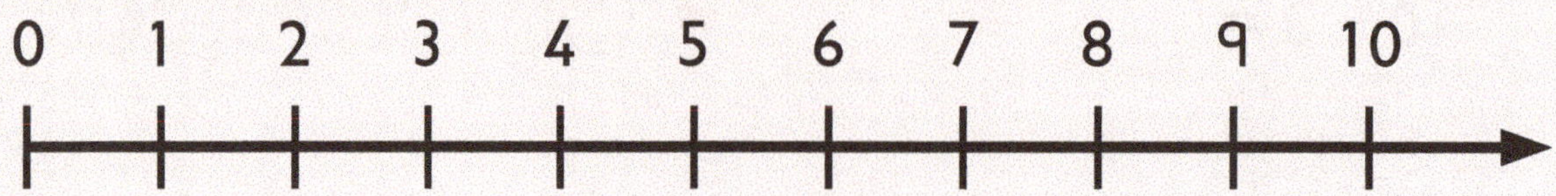

3 Write a subtraction sentence for the following questions and use a number line to count back.

(a) There are 10 cookies on a plate.

Tya eats 2 cookies.

How many cookies are left on the plate?

☐ − ☐ = ☐

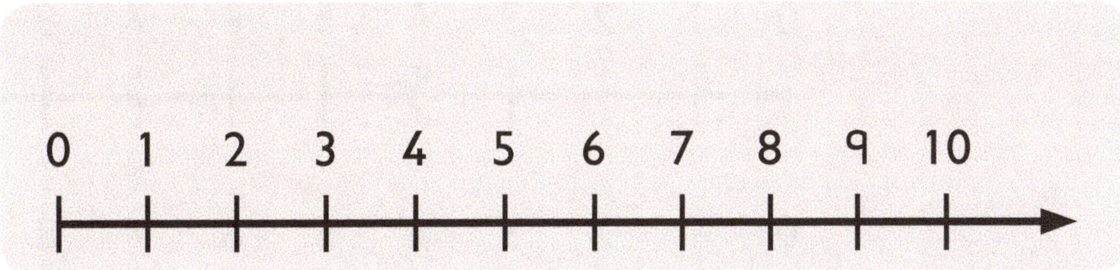

There are ☐ cookies left on the plate.

(b) I have 9 oranges.

7 oranges are taken away by my cousin.

How many oranges do I have left?

☐ − ☐ = ☐

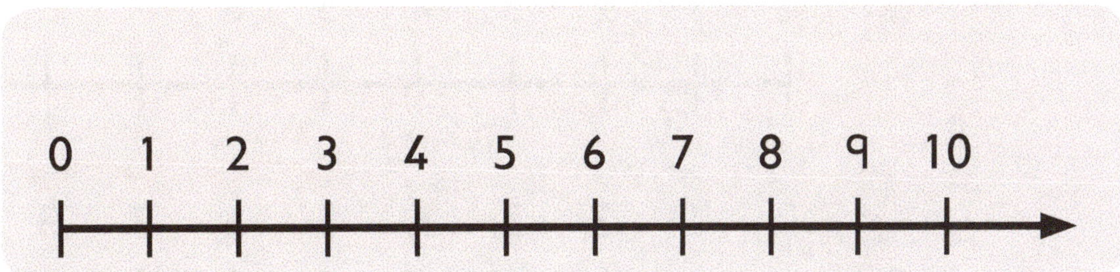

I have ☐ oranges left.

4 Look at the subtraction sentences. Tick the correct number line that matches the number sentence.

(a) $5 - 2 = 3$

☐ 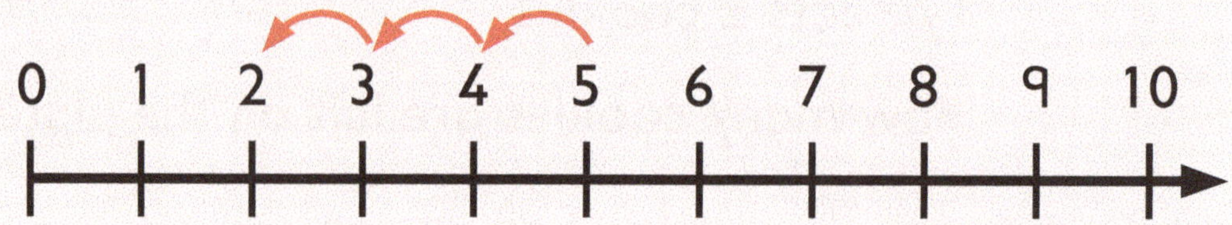

☐ 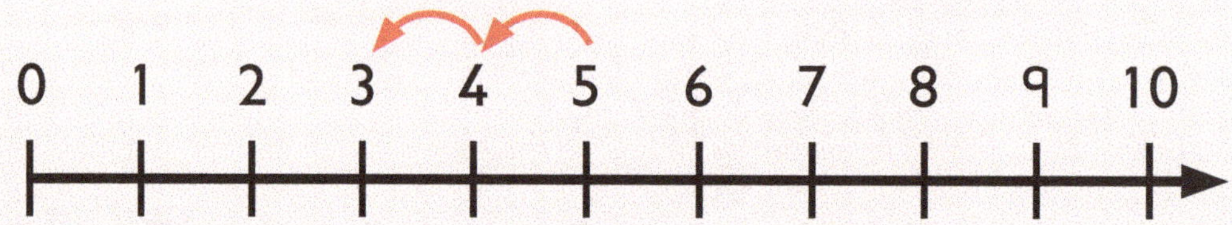

☐ 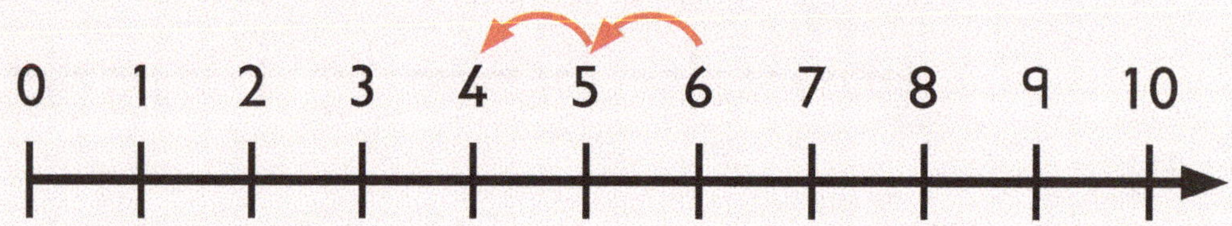

(b) $8 - 5 = 3$

☐ 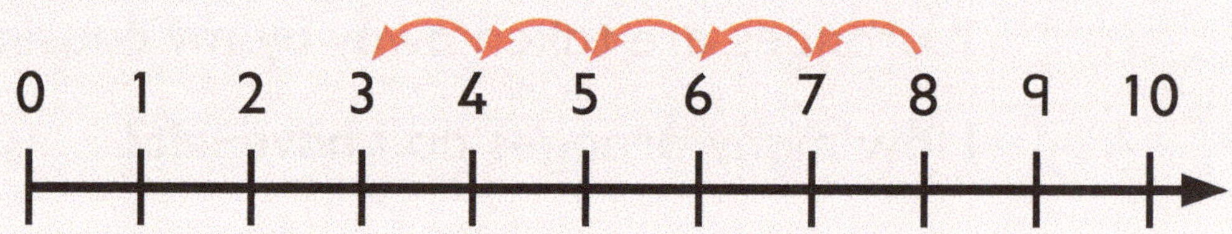

☐ 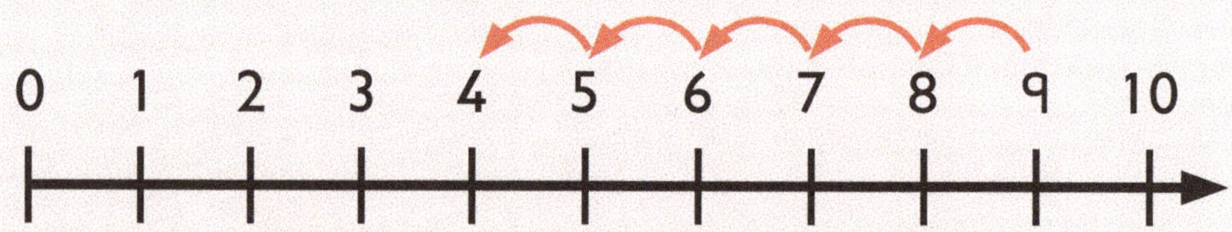

☐ 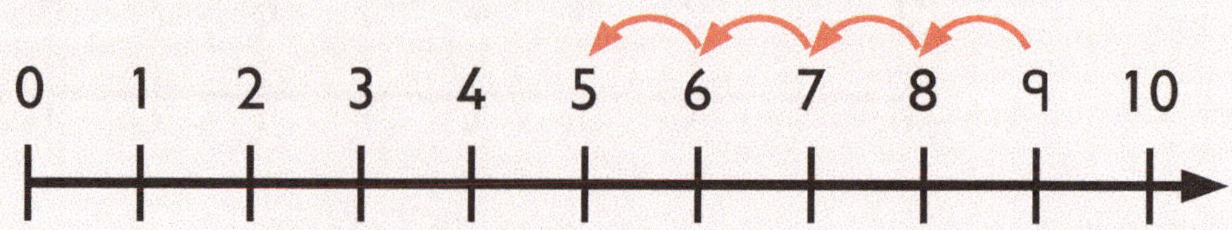

5 Read the subtraction sentences.

Count back to find the answer.

(a) 8 − 4 = ☐

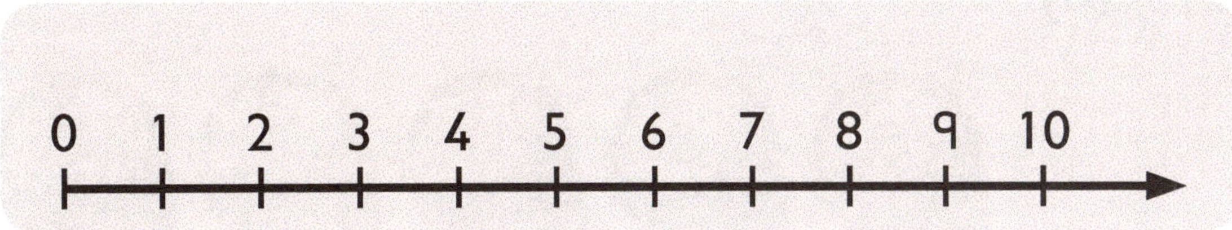

(b) 9 − 3 = ☐

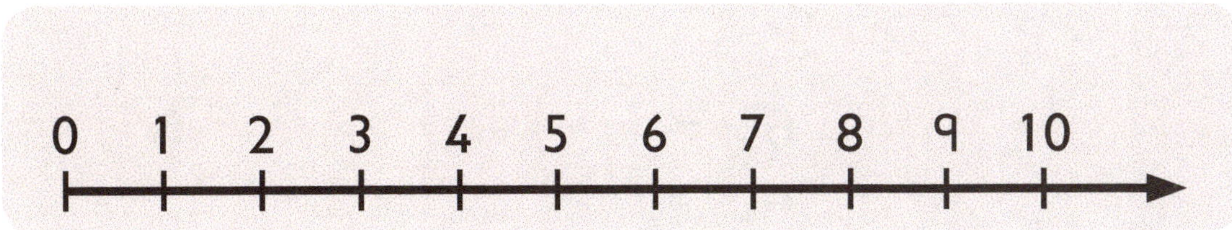

(c) 10 − 7 = ☐

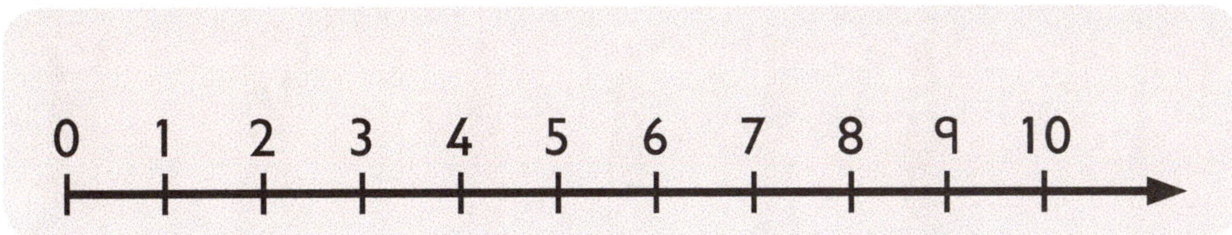

6 Complete the subtraction sentences using the count back method.

(a) 10 − 9 = ☐ **(b)** 8 − 4 = ☐

(c) 7 − 7 = ☐ **(d)** 10 − 8 = ☐

(e) 9 − 7 = ☐ **(f)** 6 − 1 = ☐

Practice 3: Subtraction using number bonds

1 Complete the subtraction sentence and number bond.

(a)

6 − ☐ = ☐

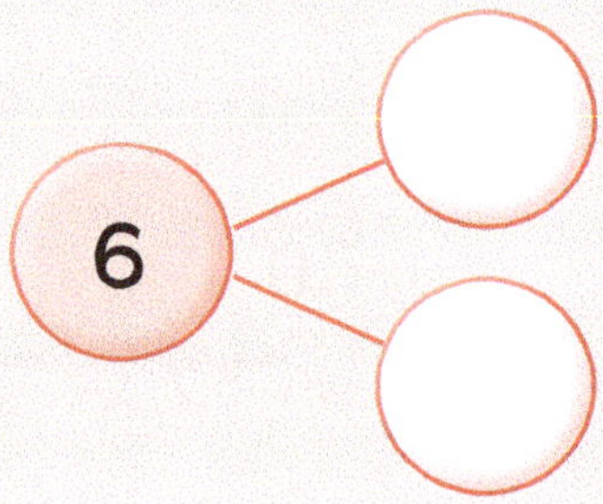

(b)

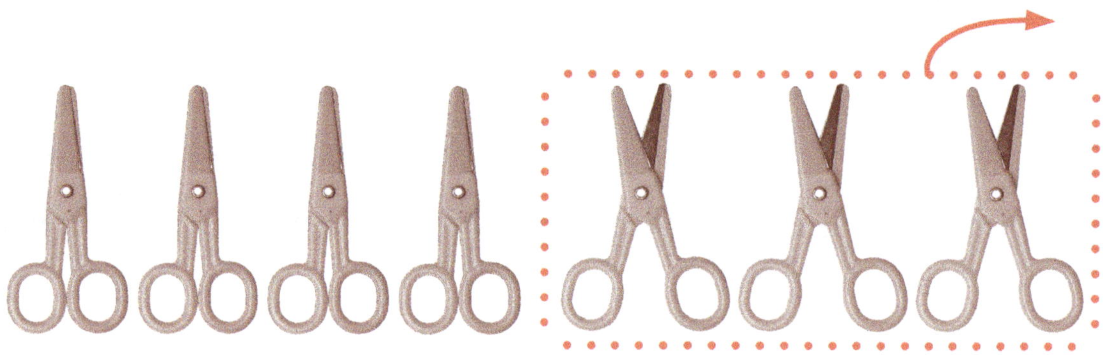

☐ − ☐ = ☐

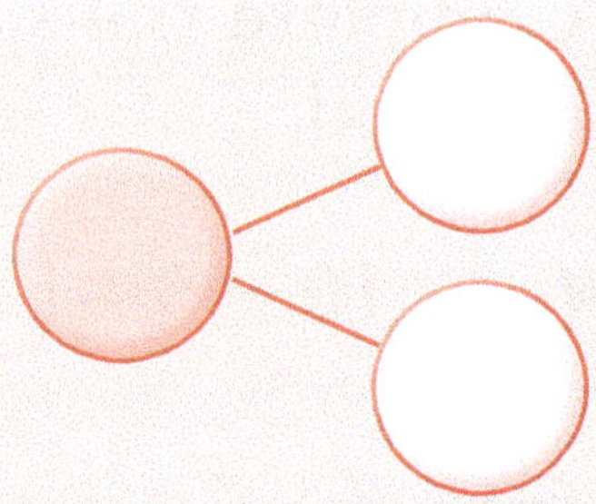

(c)

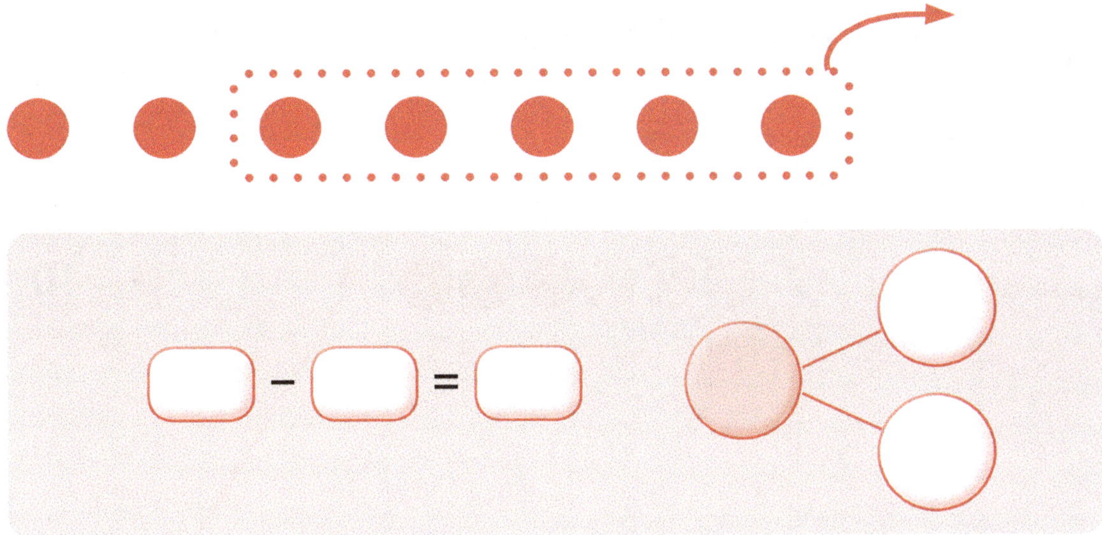

(d)

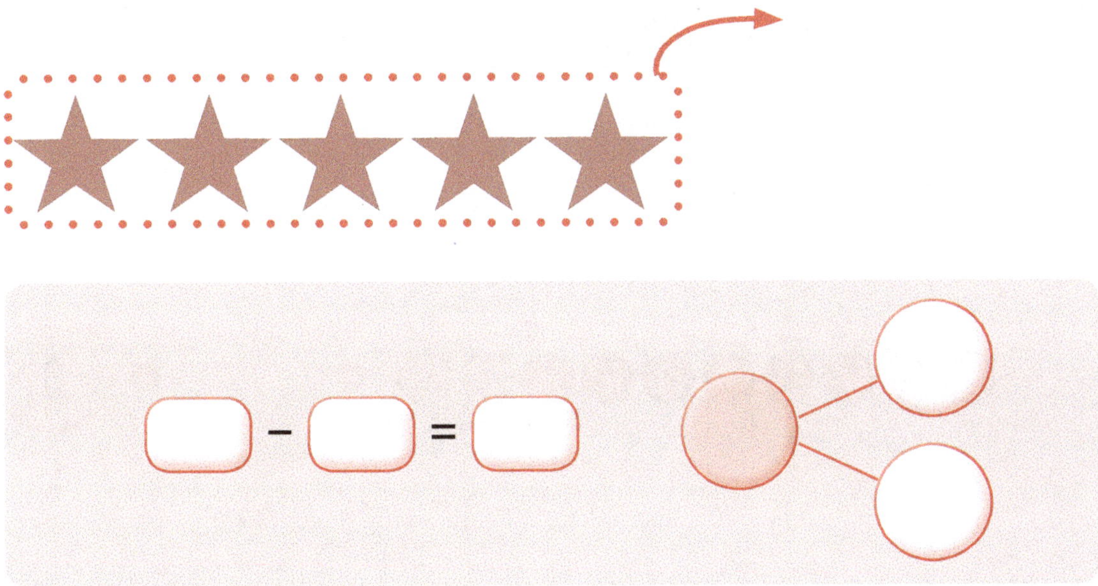

(e)

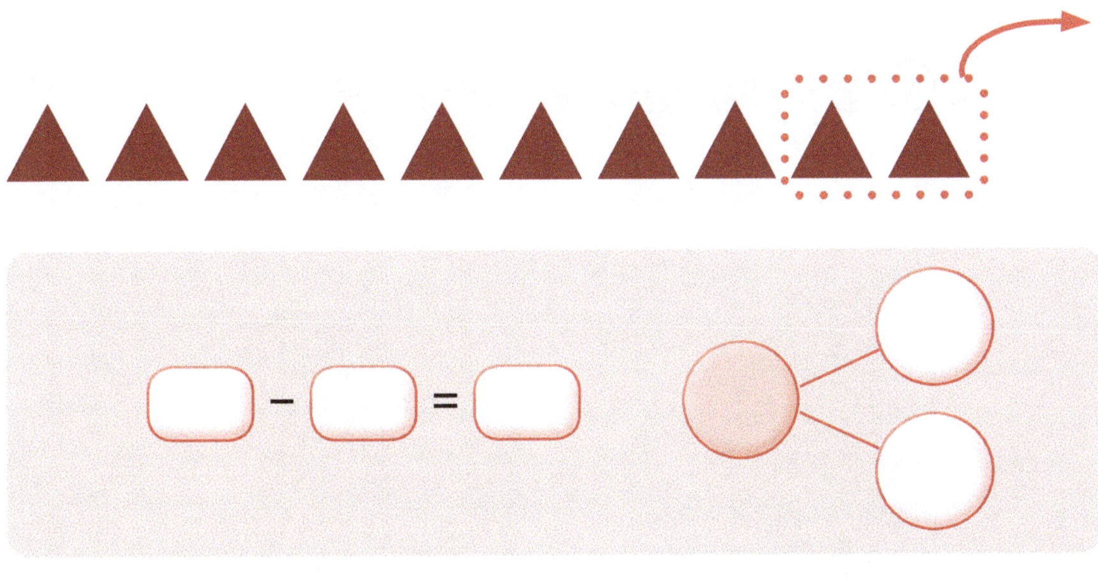

2 Match the picture to the number bond and fill in the blank.

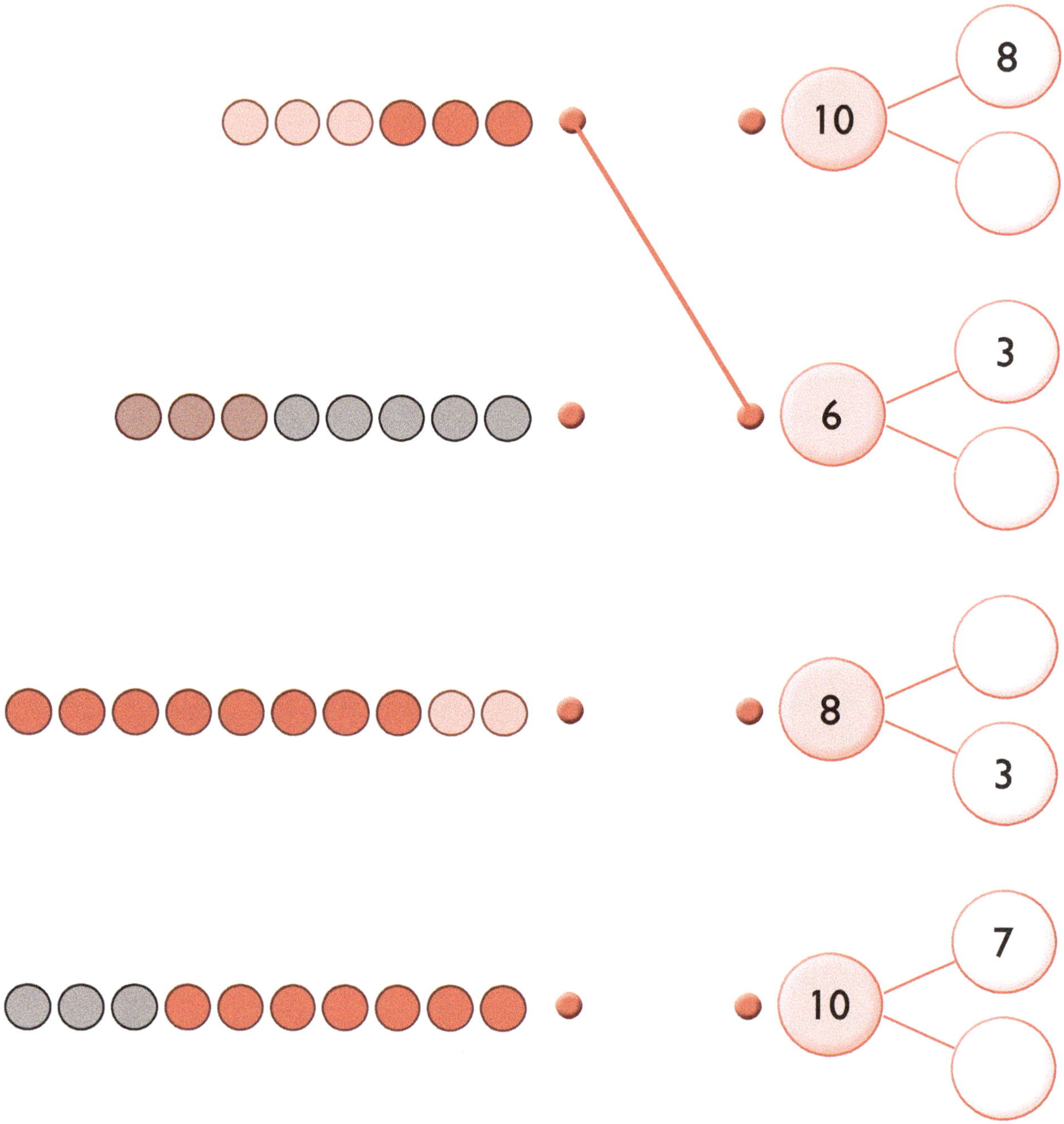

3. Complete the number bonds.

(a) 7 − 5 = [ ]

(b) 5 − 3 = [ ]

(c) 10 − 6 = [ ]

(d) 9 − 0 = [ ]

4. Match the subtraction sentence to the number bond.

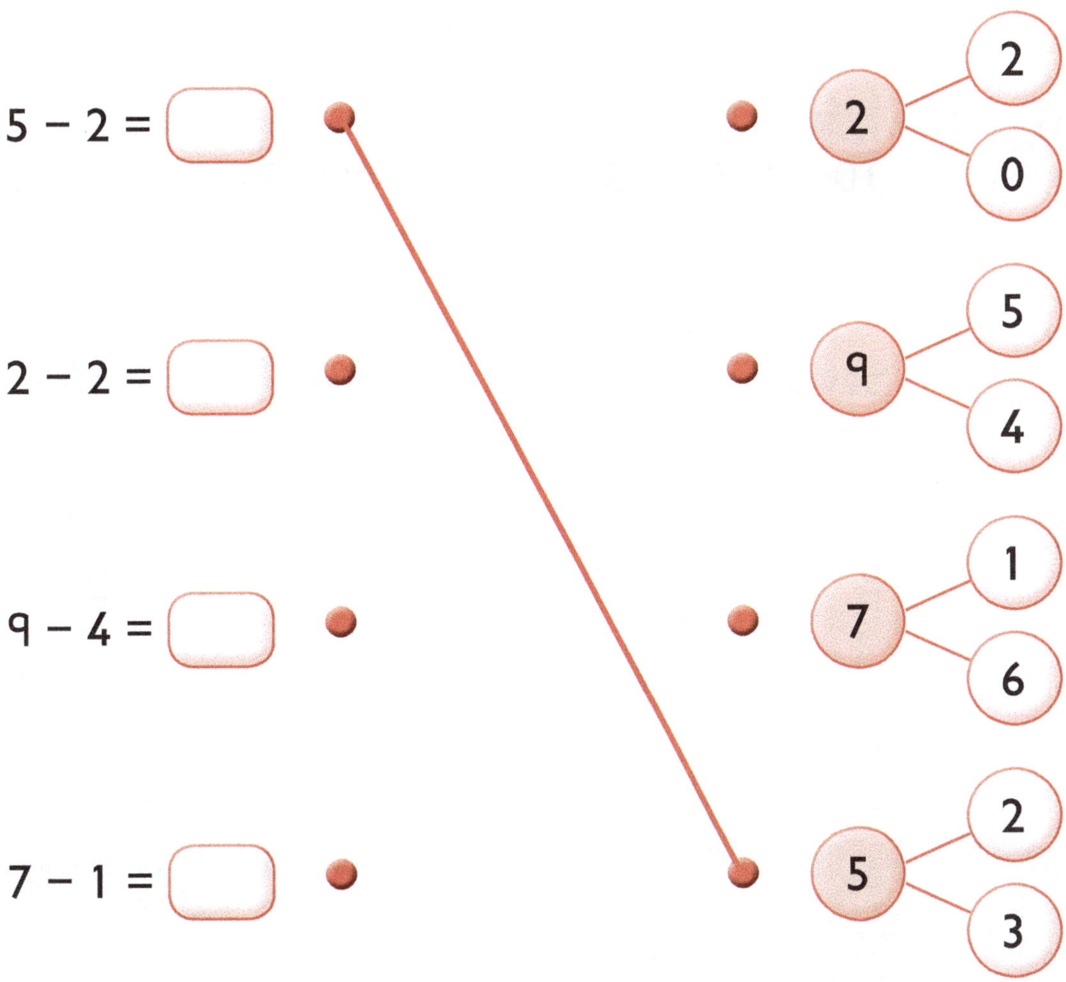

5 Tick the boxes that have the same answer.

(a)
- ☐ 4 − 3
- ☐ one
- ☐ 5 −3
- ☐ 7 − 7

(b)
- ☐ eight
- ☐ 9 − 2
- ☐ 10 − 4
- ☐ 7 − 0

(c)
- ☐ 6 − 5
- ☐ 9 − 4
- ☐ five
- ☐ 4 − 2

(d)
- ☐ 2 − 0
- ☐ 7 − 6
- ☐ 8 − 0
- ☐ two

(e)
- ☐ 10 − 5
- ☐ 5 − 1
- ☐ 8 − 3
- ☐ seven

(f)
- ☐ seven
- ☐ six
- ☐ five
- ☐ 10 − 4

(g)
- ☐ 8 − 5
- ☐ nine
- ☐ 6 − 3
- ☐ 8

6 Use the numbers and signs to form a subtraction sentence.

(a) − 8 9 = 1 | 9 − 1 = 8

(b) 6 = − 2 4

(c) = 10 10 − 0

(d) 3 − 9 6 =

(e) 1 7 8 = −

(f) 5 = − 5 0

(g) 6 7 = 13 −

Practice 4: Subtraction as 'how many more to make?'

1. Samir's mother buys 7 mangoes from the market.

   Samir finds 5 of the mangoes in a bowl.

   How many more mangoes are there to find?

   Count on from 5 to show how many more mangoes there are to find.

☐ – ☐ = ☐

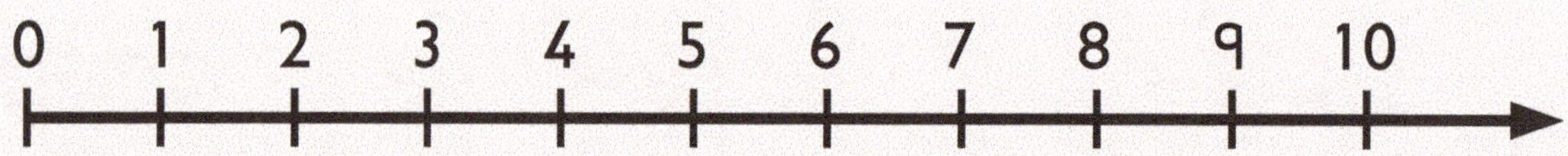

2. A jar holds 8 cookies.

   There are 5 cookies in the jar.

   How many more cookies can be put in the jar?

☐ – ☐ = ☐

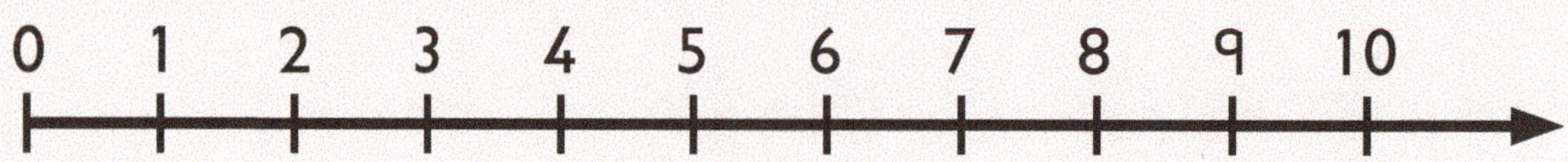

3 Write a subtraction sentence for the following questions and use a number line to count on.

(a) Jade has put 5 cupcakes on the cake stand.

Her mother wants 10 cupcakes on the cake stand.

How many more cupcakes should Jade put on the cake stand?

☐ − ☐ = ☐

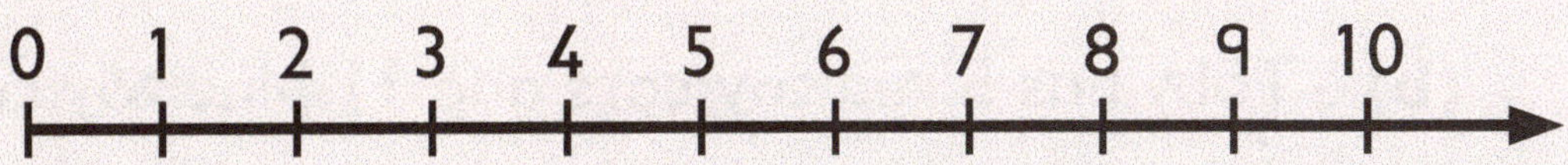

Jade should put ☐ more cupcakes on the cake stand.

(b) Samir puts 6 marbles into a bag.

Tya puts some more marbles into the bag.

There are 9 marbles in the bag now.

How many marbles did Tya put into the bag?

☐ − ☐ = ☐

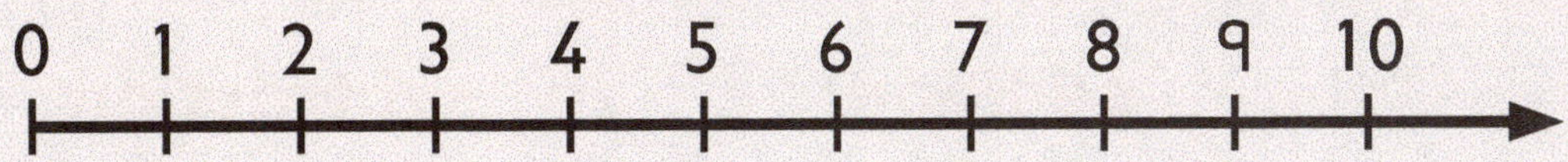

Tya put ☐ marbles into the bag.

Practice 5: Subtraction and addition word problems

1 Read each word problem. Is it an addition or subtraction word problem? Circle the type of problem.

(a) Jade has 12 old books and 6 new books.

How many books does she have altogether?

addition subtraction

(b) Toby has 5 red toy cars and 11 blue toy cars.

How many cars does Toby have altogether?

addition subtraction

(c) Tya has 15 cookies. She gives 7 cookies to Padma.

How many cookies does Tya have left?

addition subtraction

(d) There are 12 apples on a tree. Samir picks 4 apples.

How many apples are left on the tree?

addition subtraction

2 Solve the word problems.

(a) Han has 13 walnuts. He gives 3 walnuts to Samir.

How many walnuts does Han have now?

13 − ☐ = ☐

Han has ☐ walnuts now.

(b) There are 16 padlocks. 5 get locked.

How many padlocks are unlocked?

16 ☐ ☐ ☐ ☐

☐ padlocks are unlocked.

(c) There are 14 birds. 4 fly away.

How many birds are left?

There are ☐ birds left.

(d) Tya has 16 biscuits. She eats 3 of them.

How many biscuits does Tya have left?

Tya has ☐ biscuits left.

(e) Toby has 15 cubes. Han gives him another 4.

How many cubes does Toby have now?

☐ ☐ ☐ ☐ ☐

Toby has ☐ cubes altogether now.

3 Look at the pictures and write your own word problem.

(a) ☐

☐

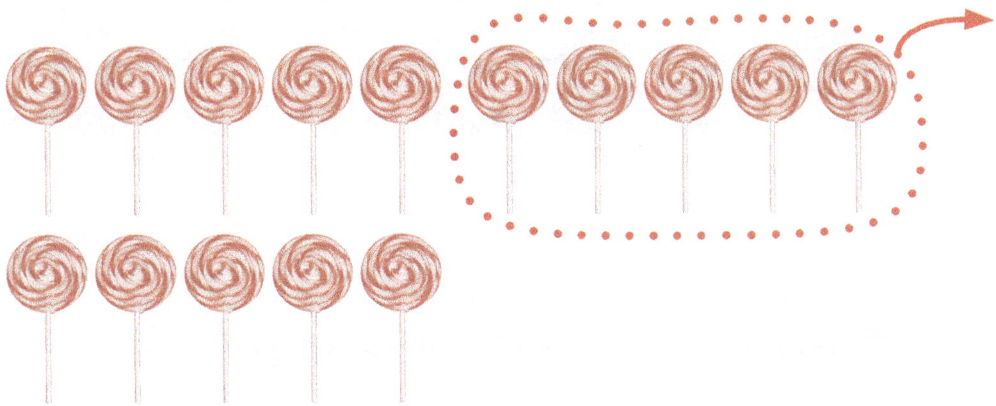

☐ ☐ ☐ ☐ ☐

There are ☐ lollipops left.

(b)

There are ☐ peppers altogether.

(c)

There are ☐ balls altogether.

4. Solve the following word problems.

(a) My sister received 8 presents at her party.

I received 11 presents at my party.

How many more presents did I receive?

☐ ☐ ☐ ☐ ☐

I received ☐ more presents than my sister.

(b) I ate 13 peanuts.

My brother ate 4 fewer peanuts.

How many peanuts did my brother eat?

☐ ☐ ☐ ☐ ☐

My brother ate ☐ peanuts.

4 Shapes and geometric reasoning

Practice 1: 2D shapes

1. Match the pictures that are of the same shape.

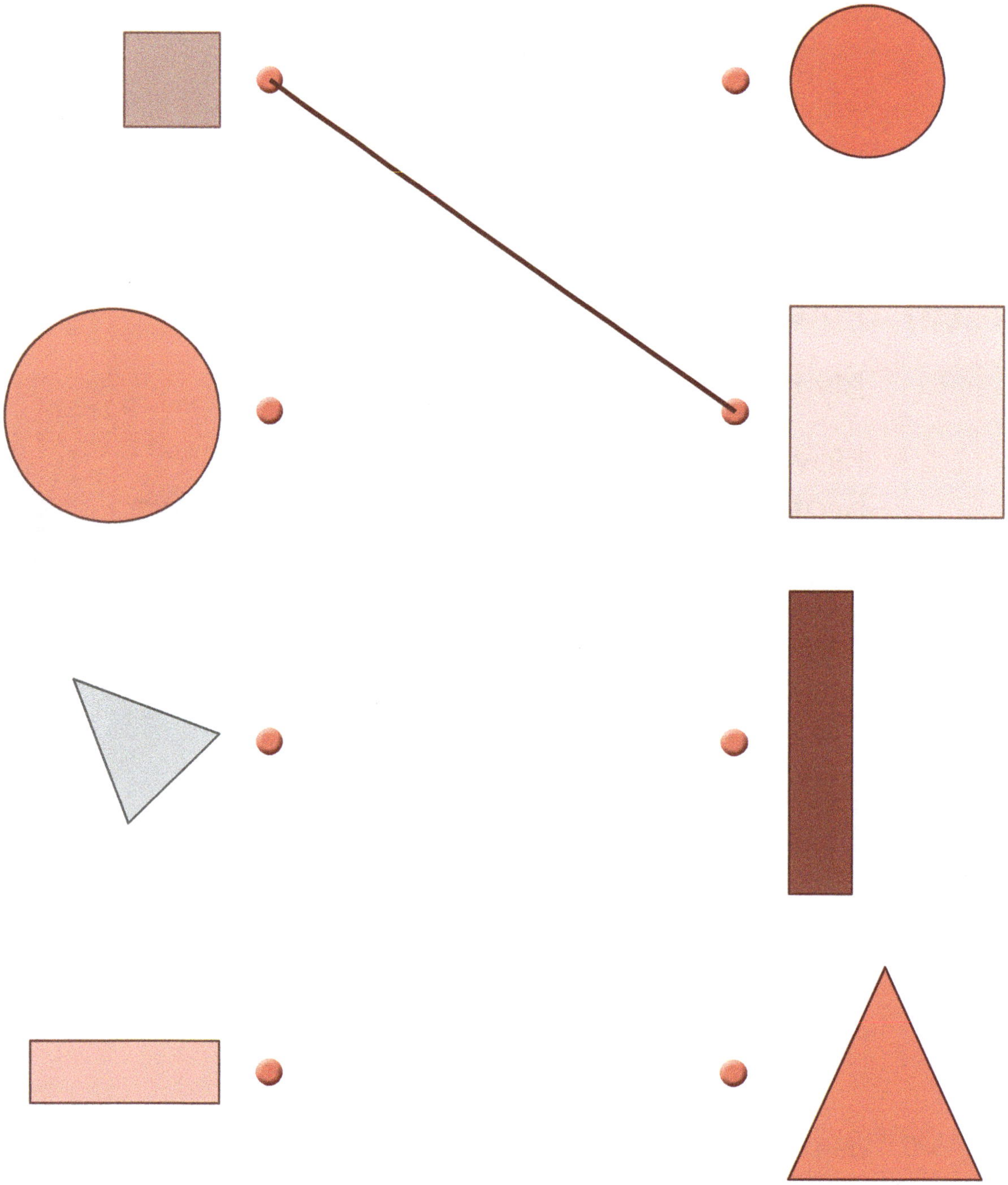

2 Circle the name of the shape.

	square	triangle	rectangle	circle
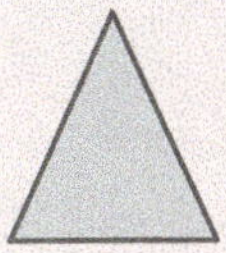	square	triangle	rectangle	circle
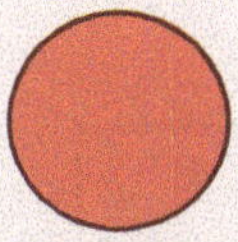	square	triangle	rectangle	circle
	square	triangle	rectangle	circle

3 Look at the pictures. Write down the name of the shape you see.

4 Look at the shapes.

Colour the circles green.

Colour the squares red.

Colour the rectangles blue.

Colour the triangles yellow.

5 Colour the shapes that are the same shape as the black shape.

(a)

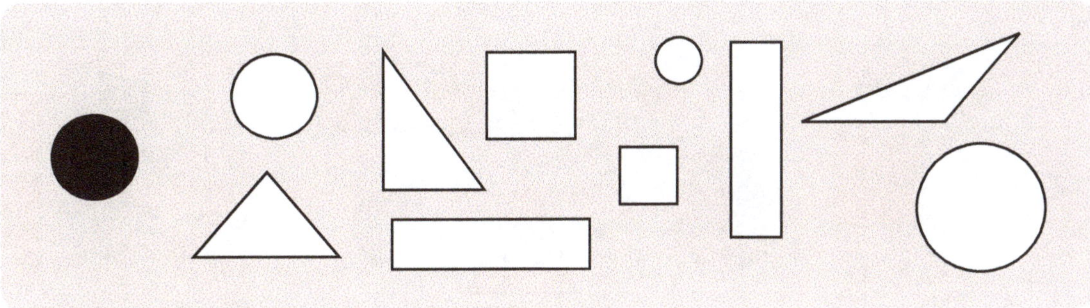

(b)

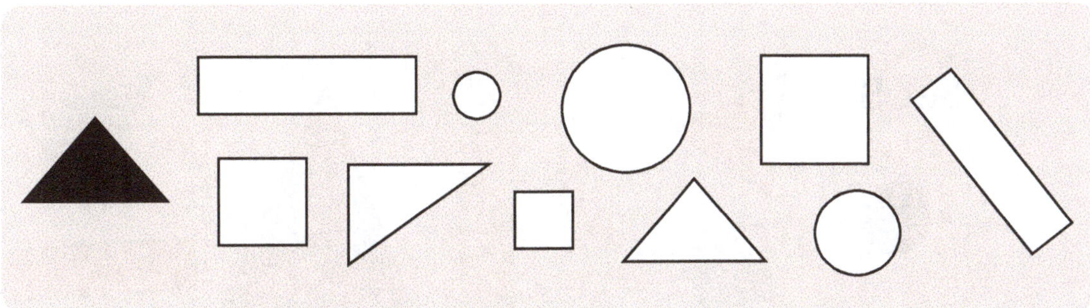

(c)

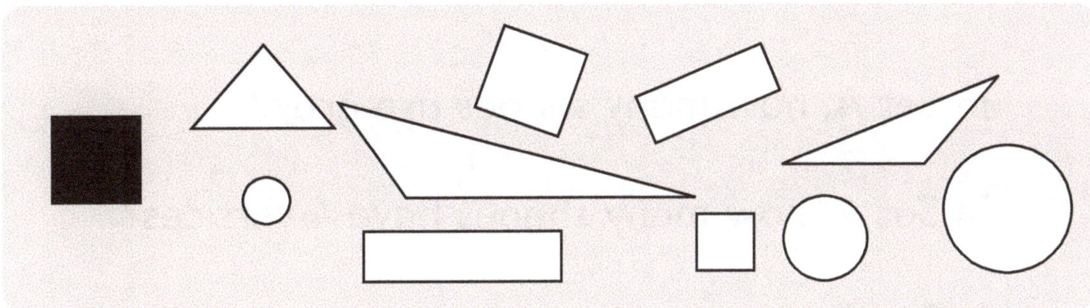

(d)

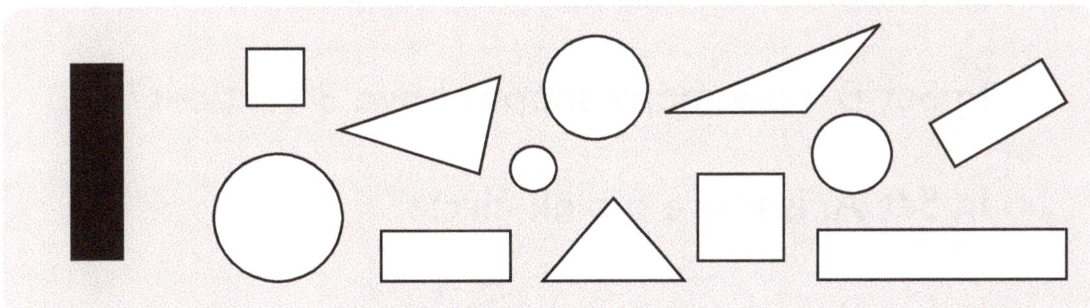

6 Look at Set A and Set B.

Answer the questions.

Set A

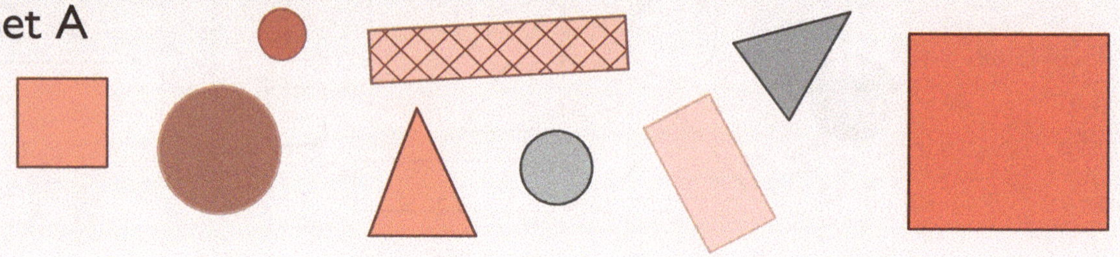

Set B

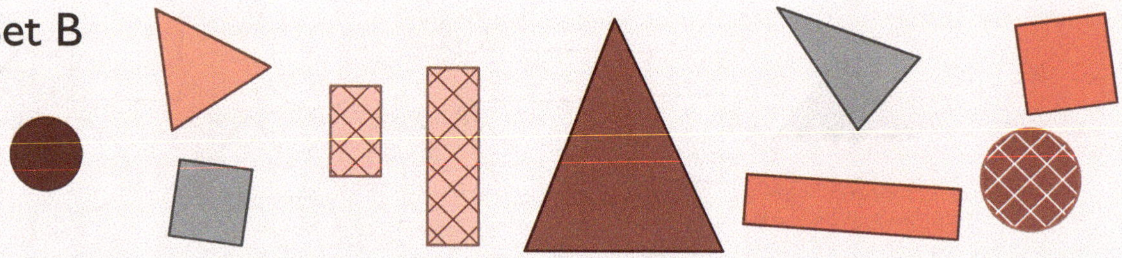

In Set A, how many shapes are grey? [ ]

In Set A, how many shapes have 4 vertices? [ ]

In Set B, how many shapes are patterned? [ ]

In Set B, how many shapes have 3 vertices? [ ]

In Set A, is there a pink circle? [ ]

In Set B, is there a red triangle? [ ]

In Set A, how many shapes have 3 sides? [ ]

In Set B, how many shapes have 4 sides? [ ]

Practice 2: Shapes and pictures

1 Look at the pictures made up of different shapes.

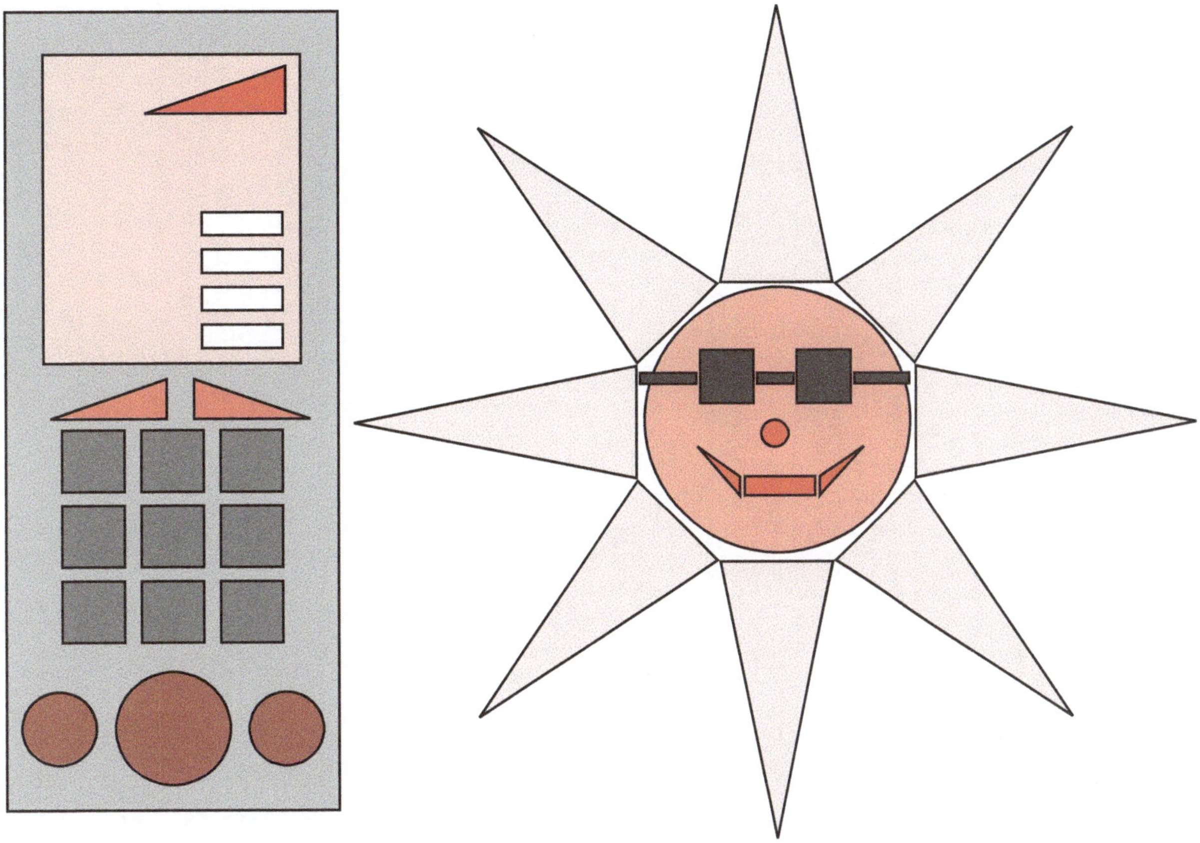

How many squares are in the phone?

How many triangles are in the Sun?

Are there more squares than rectangles in the Sun?

Which picture has more rectangles?

How many circles are there altogether?

2 Make a picture using squares, rectangles, triangles and circles. Write how many of each shape you used.

Squares ☐ Rectangles ☐ Triangles ☐ Circles ☐

Practice 3: Grouping shapes

1 Look at the sets of shapes. Tick how they are grouped.

(a)

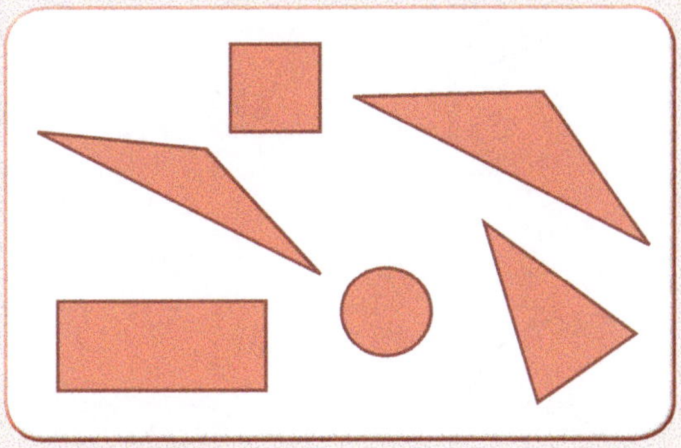

☐ by shape
☐ by colour
☐ by size
☐ number of vertices
☐ number of sides

(b)

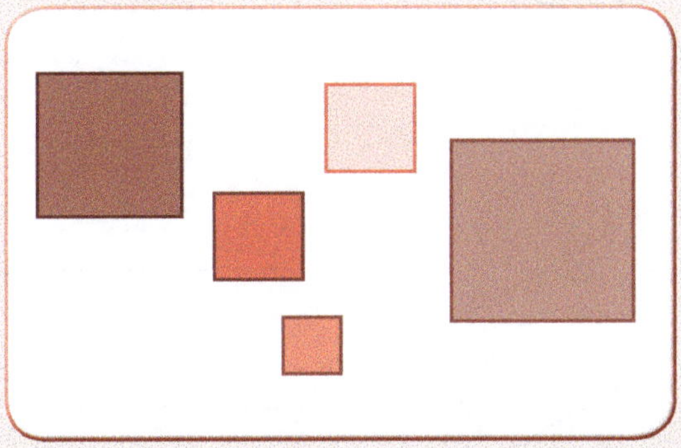

☐ by shape
☐ by colour
☐ by size
☐ number of vertices
☐ number of sides

(c)

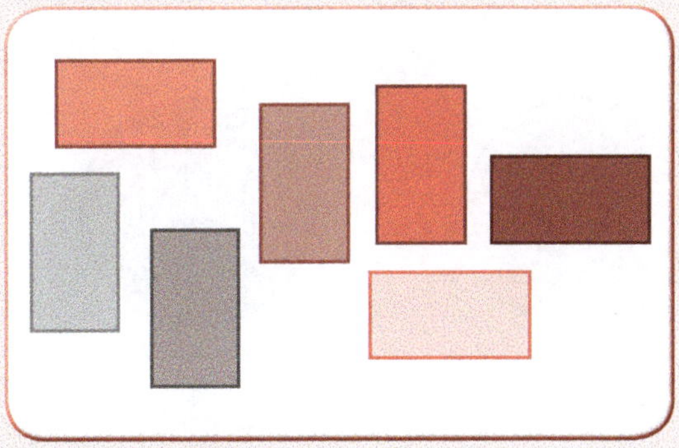

☐ by shape
☐ by colour
☐ by size
☐ number of vertices
☐ number of sides

(d)

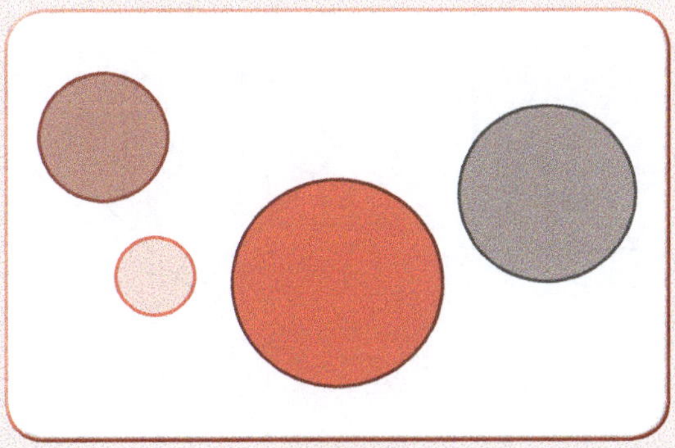

☐ by shape
☐ by colour
☐ by size
☐ number of vertices
☐ number of sides

2 Circle the shape that does not belong to the group.

(a)

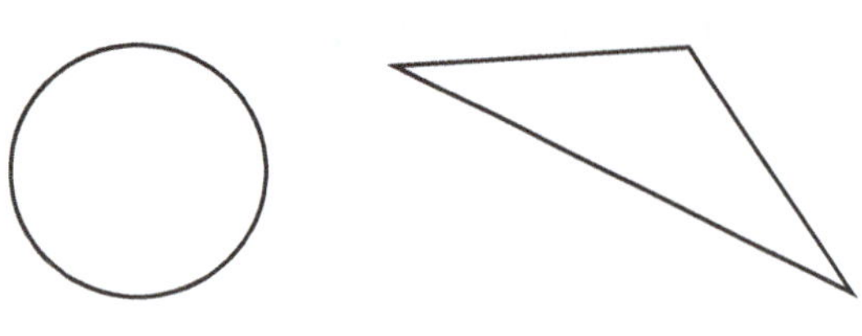

(b)

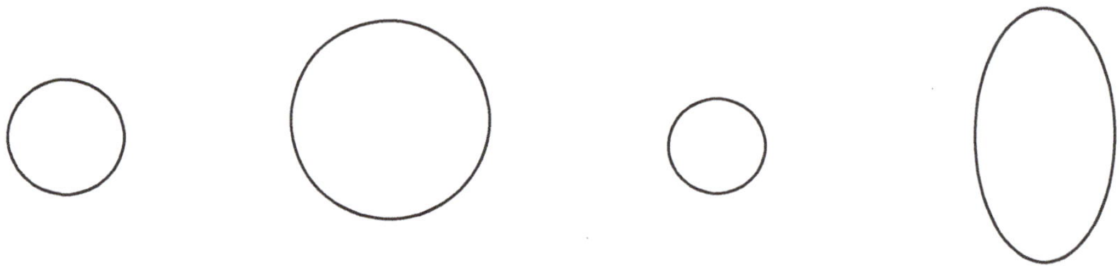

(c)

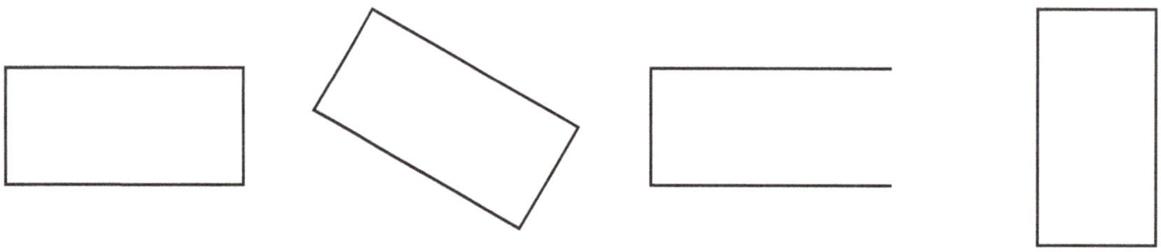

(d)

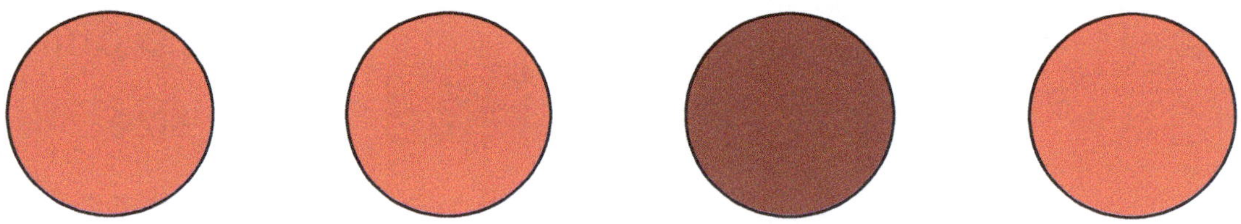

(e)

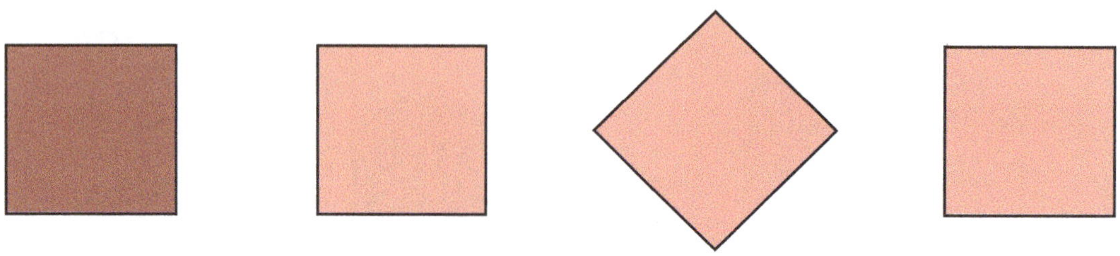

3. Toby grouped 8 shapes as shown below.

Circle the correct answers.

(a) The shapes in Group A are (**big** / **small**) and (**red** / **grey**).

(b) The shapes in Group B are (**big** / **small**) and (**red** / **grey**).

(c) The shapes in Group C are (**big** / **small**) and (**red** / **grey**).

(d) The shapes in Group D are (**big** / **small**) and (**red** / **grey**).

4 Make 2 groups of circles that are grouped by **size**.

5 Make 2 groups of shapes that are grouped by **colour**.

6 Make 2 groups of shapes that are grouped by **shape**.

Practice 4: Patterns with shapes

1. Circle the shape that comes next in the pattern.

(a)

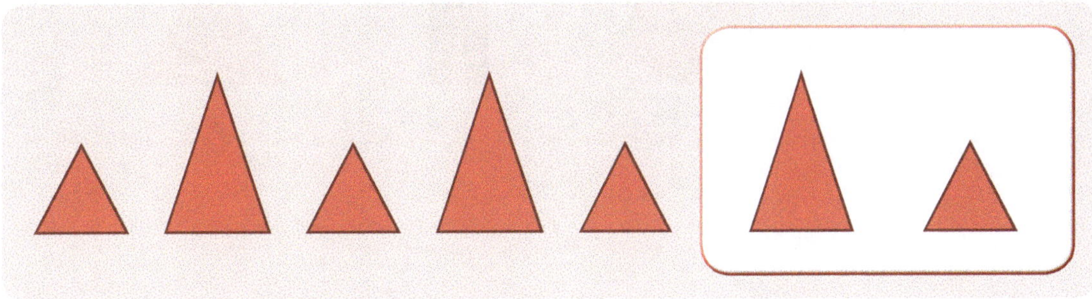

(b)

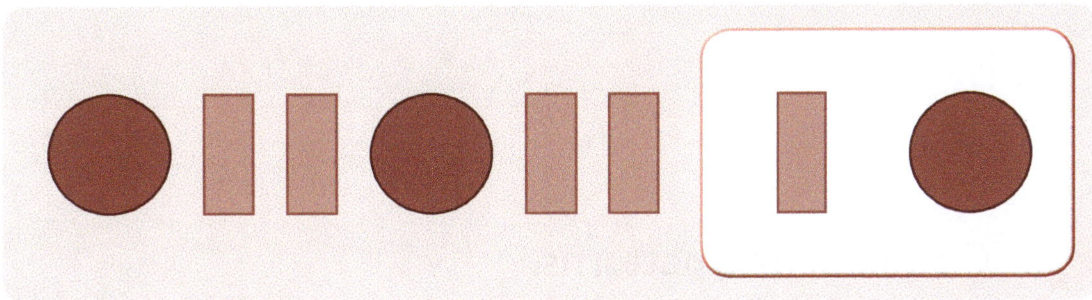

(c)

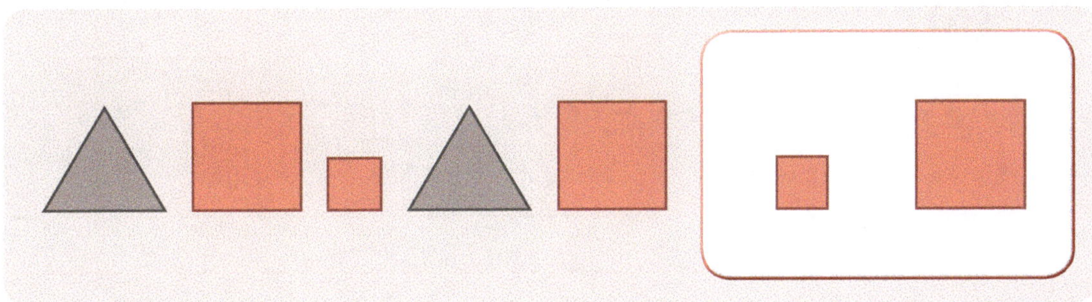

(d)

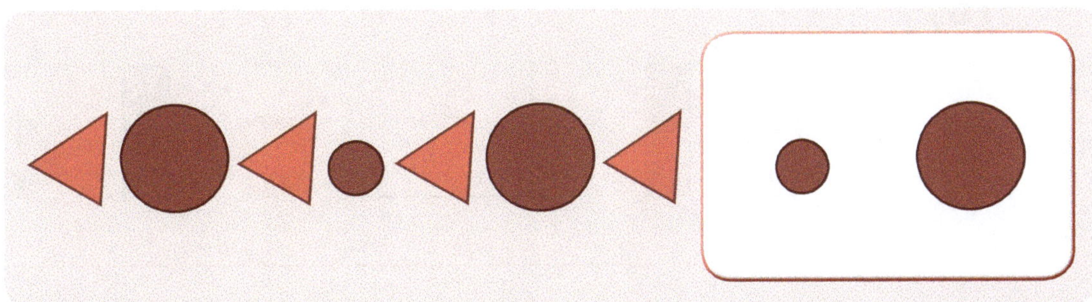

(e)

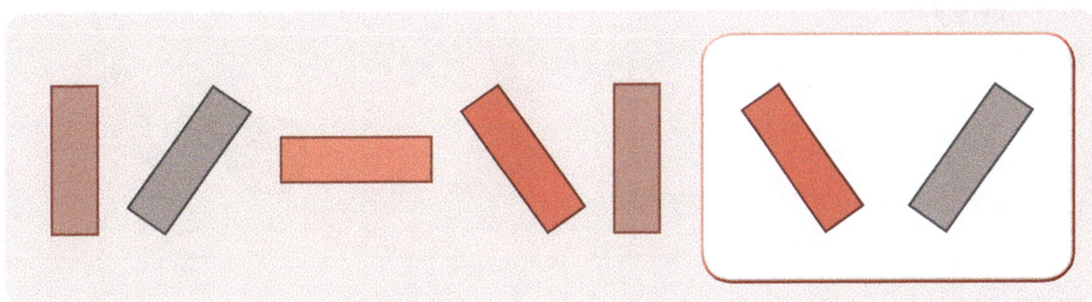

2 Draw a pattern using 2 of the shapes below.

3 Complete the patterns.

(a)

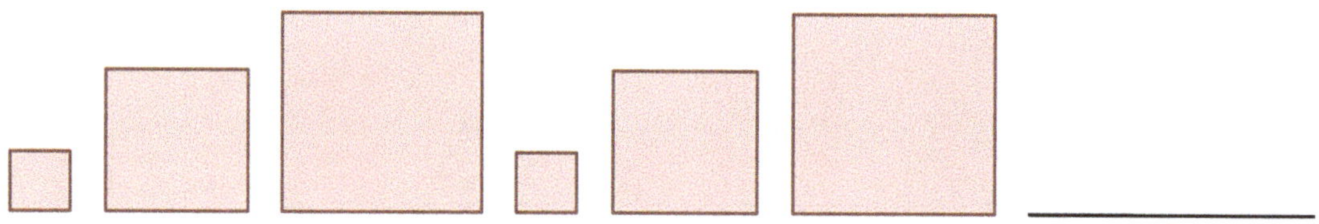

(b)

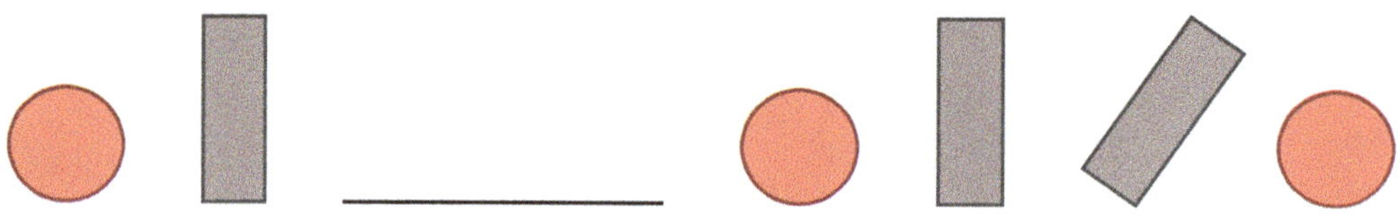

(c)

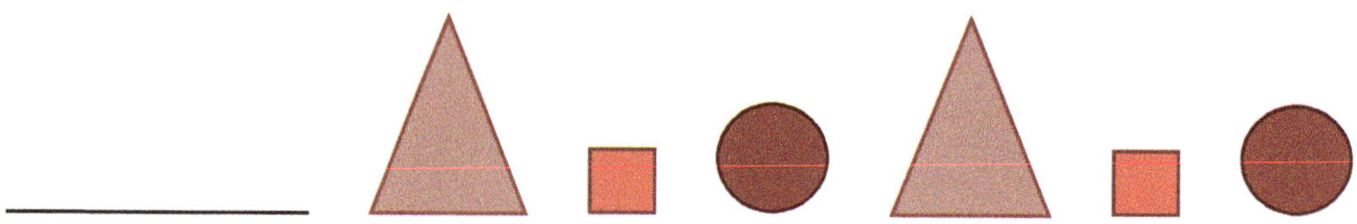

4 Cut out the shapes and make a pattern by sticking them in the box below.

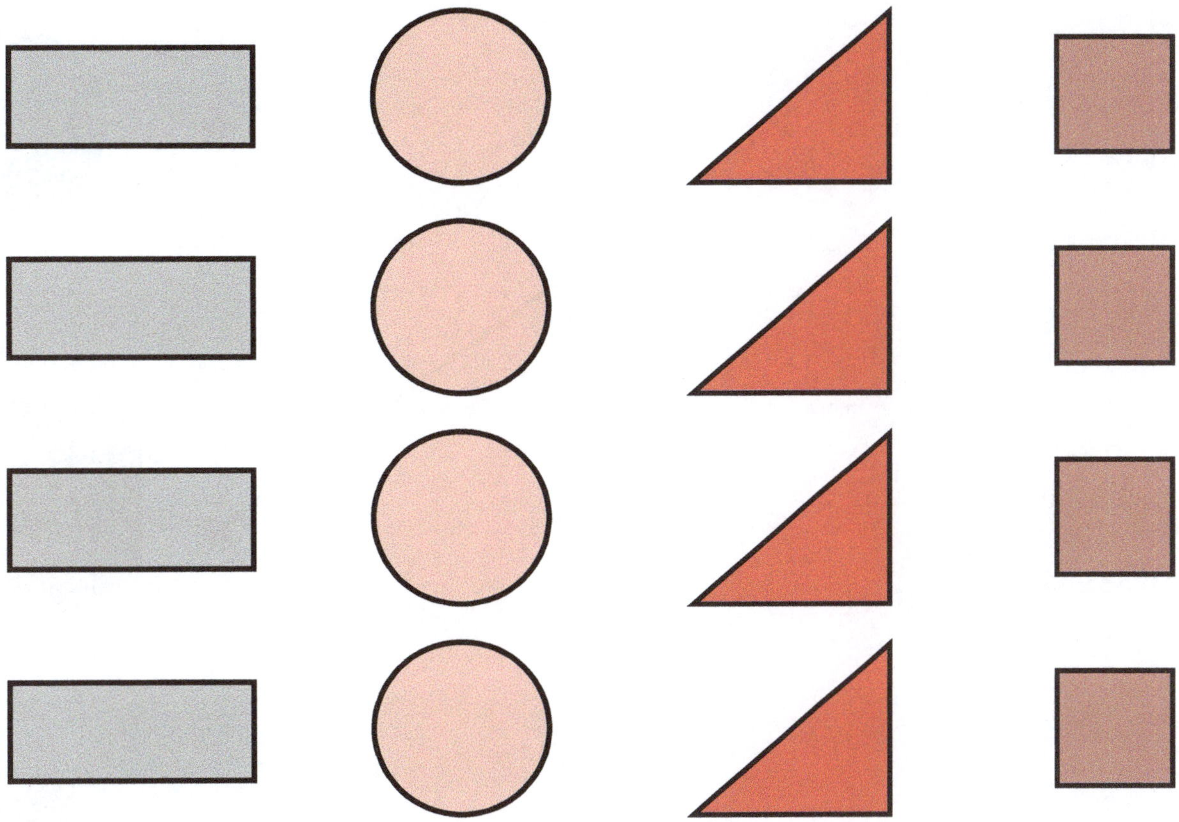

Practice 5: 3D shapes

1 Match the shapes that are the same.

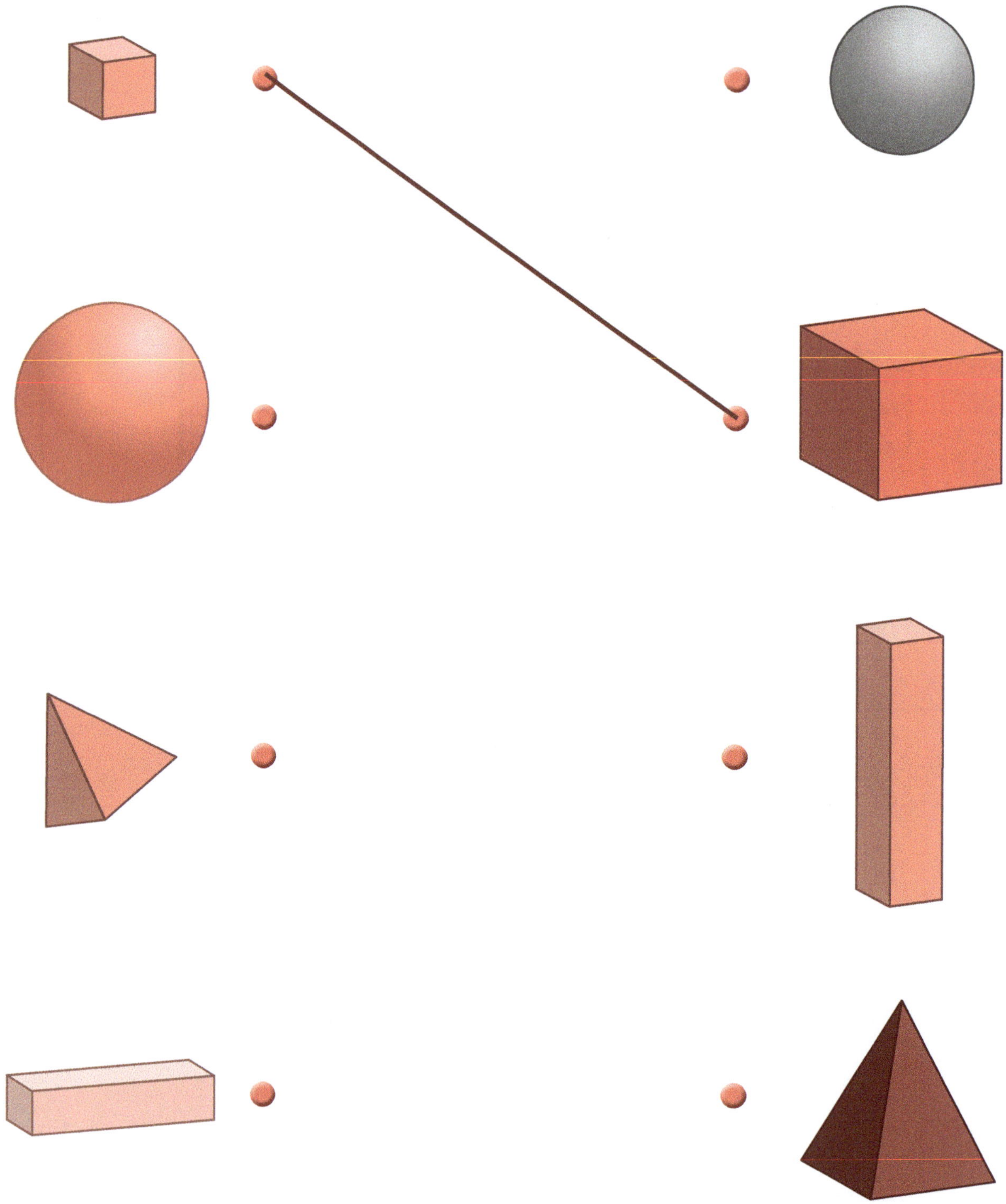

2 Circle the name of the 3D shape.

(a)  cylinder sphere pyramid cone

(b) 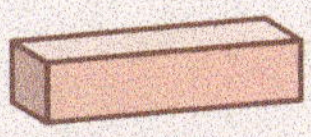 cube cuboid sphere cylinder

(c) 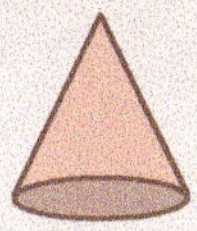 pyramid cube sphere cone

(d) 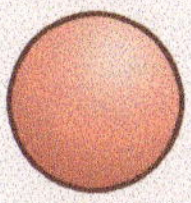 cylinder pyramid sphere cone

(e) 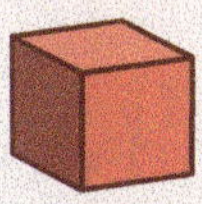 cube cuboid sphere cylinder

(f) 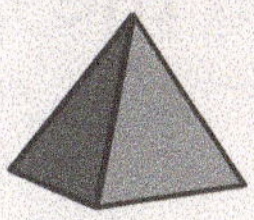 cone cube pyramid cuboid

3 Look at the pictures. Write down the name of the 3D shape you see.

(a) 

(b) 

(c) 

(d) 

(e) 

(f) 

4 Toby finds an eraser in his pencil case. He draws a picture of the eraser and names the 3D shape it looks similar to.

Look around your home or classroom. Find objects that look similar to 3D shapes. Draw and label the objects below and on the opposite page.

cubes

cuboids

spheres

cones

cylinders

5 Look at the 3D shapes.

Colour the cubes green.

Colour the cuboids blue.

Colour the pyramids yellow.

Colour the spheres red.

Colour the cones orange.

Colour the cylinders purple.

Practice 6: Recognising line symmetry

1 Circle the shapes that have one line of symmetry.

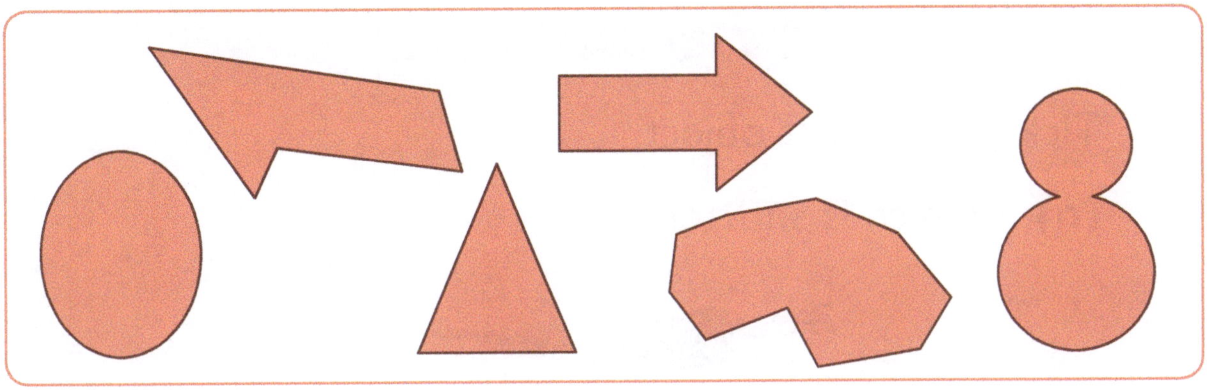

2 Draw where the line of symmetry is on these shapes.

3 Colour half of each of these shapes.

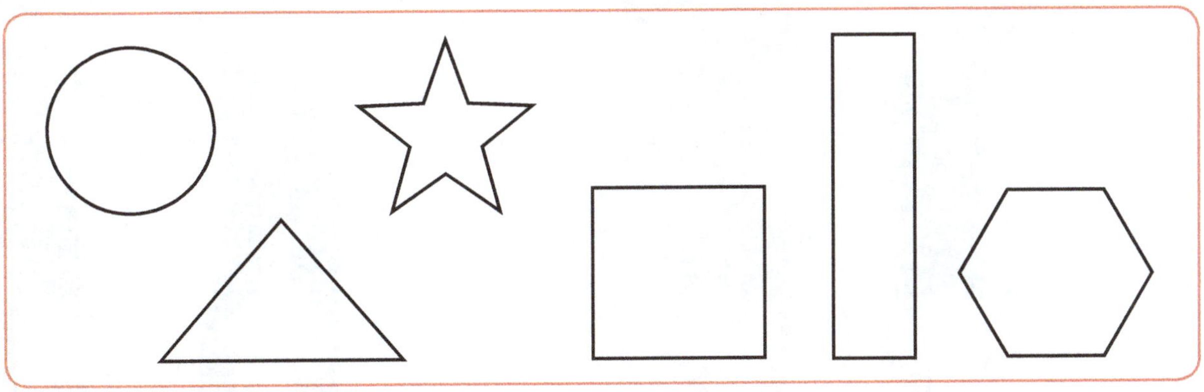

5 Length

Practice 1: Comparing the length of two objects

1. Tick the correct object.

(a) Which is shorter?

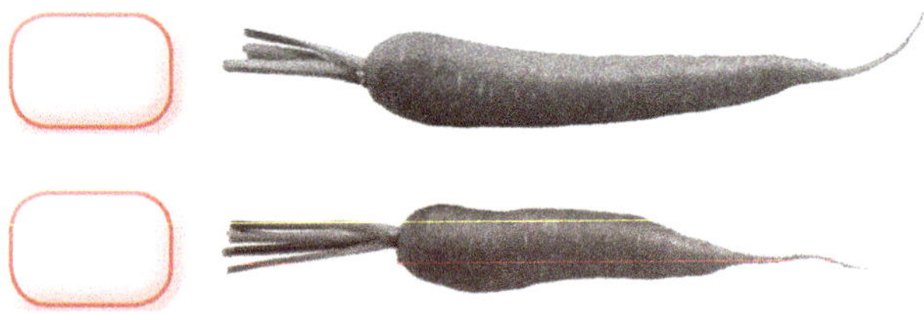

(b) Which is shorter?

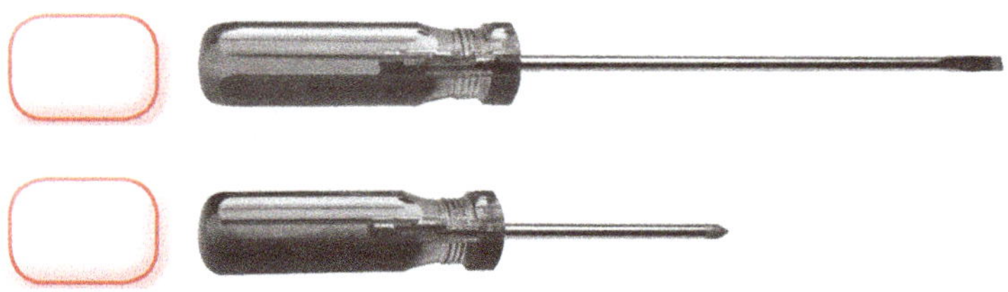

(c) Who is taller?

(d) Who is shorter?

(e) Which is higher?

☐ ☐

2 Use the words in the box to complete the sentences.

(a)

taller	shorter

The cat is ☐ than the kitten.

The kitten is ☐ than the cat.

(b)

longer shorter

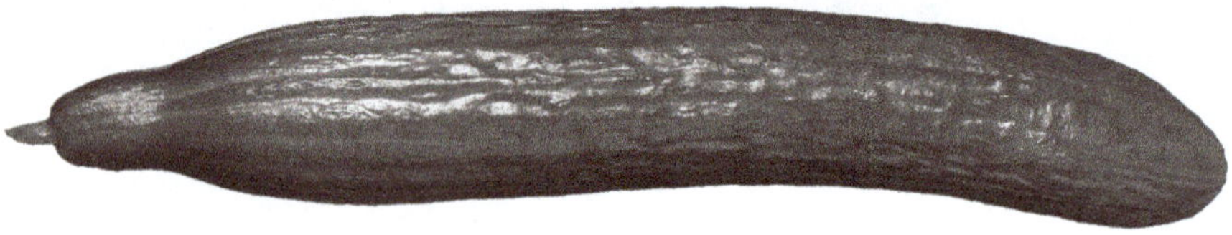

cucumber

chilli

The cucumber is [ ] than the chilli.

The chilli is [ ] than the cucumber.

(c)

higher longer taller

Padma is [ ] than Samir.

Padma

Samir

Practice 2: Comparing the length of more than two objects

1. Tick the correct object.

(a) Which is the longest?

(b) Which is the tallest?

(c) Which is the highest?

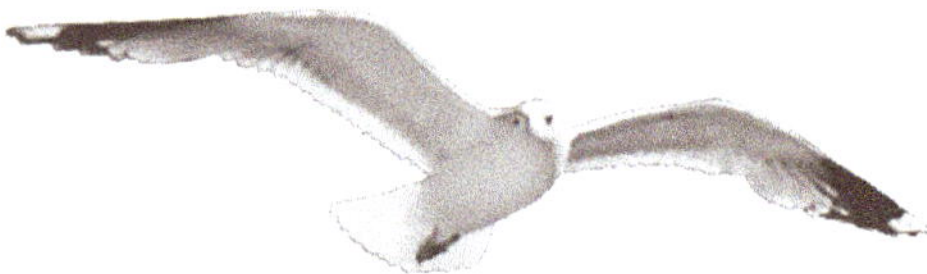

2 Tick the correct object.

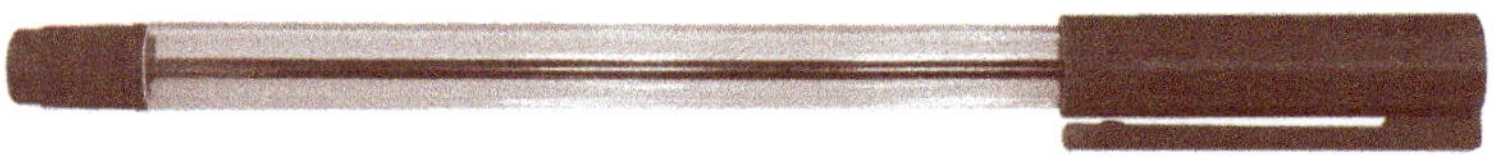

A

B

C

(a) ☐ and ☐ are longer than B.

(b) ☐ is longer than A.

(c) ☐ is the longest.

3. Fill in the blanks.

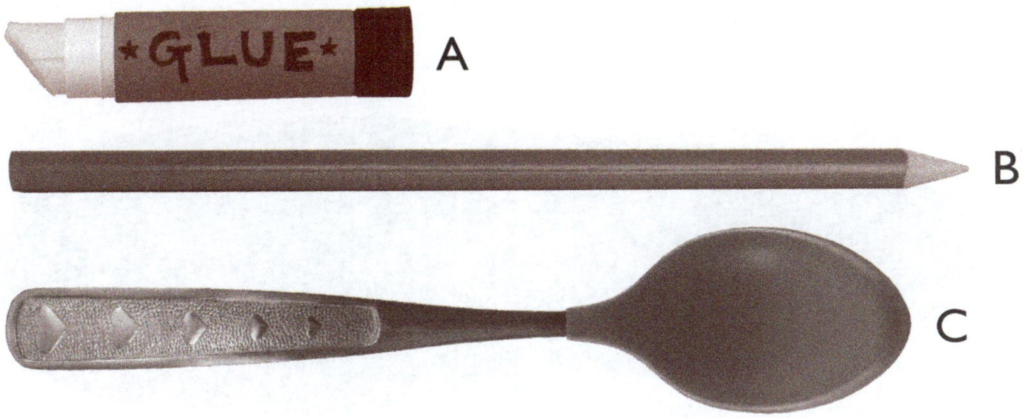

(a) ☐ and ☐ are shorter than B.

(b) ☐ is shorter than C.

(c) ☐ is the shortest.

4. Fill in the blanks.

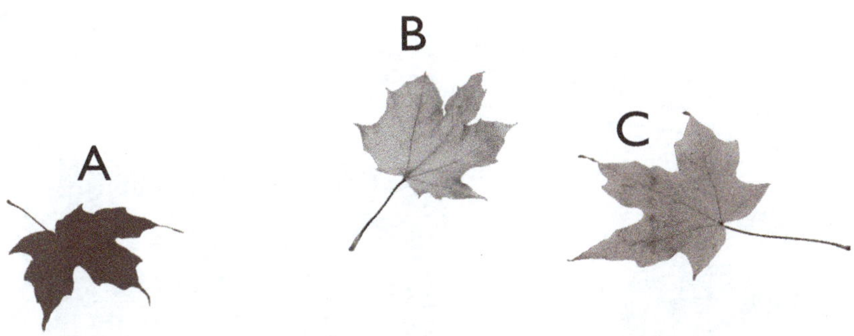

(a) ☐ and ☐ are higher than A.

(b) ☐ is higher than C.

(c) ☐ is the highest.

Practice 3: Measuring length

1 How long is each object?

(a)

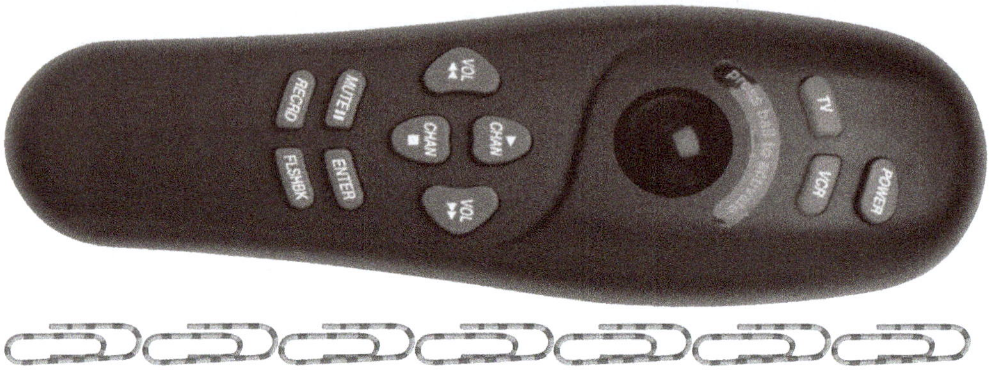

☐  long.

(b)

☐  long.

(c) ☐  long.

(d)

☐ long.

(e)

☐ long.

(f)

☐ long.

2 Use 10¢ to measure the length of each object below.

(a) 

This brush is about ☐ 10¢ long.

(b)

This toy car is about ☐ 10¢ long.

(c)

This comb is about ☐ 10¢ long.

(d) 

This pen is about ☐ 10¢ long.

3 Estimate how long each stick is. Use 10¢ to measure.

(a) 

Estimate: ☐ 10¢ long.

Actual measurement: ☐ 10¢ long.

(b) 

Estimate: ☐ 10¢ long.

Actual measurement: ☐ 10¢ long.

(c) 

Estimate: ☐ 10¢ long.

Actual measurement: ☐ 10¢ long.

(d) 

Estimate: ☐ 10¢ long.

Actual measurement: ☐ 10¢ long.

Practice 4: Measuring length in units

1 How many units long is each object?

(a)  = 1 unit

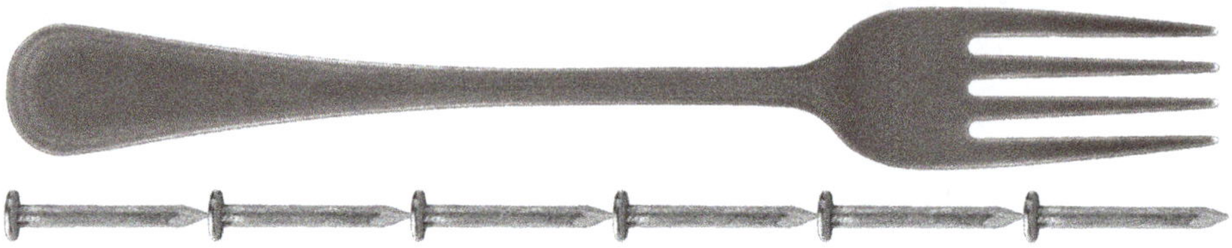

The fork is ☐ units long.

(b)  = 1 unit

The knife is ☐ units long.

(c)  = 1 unit

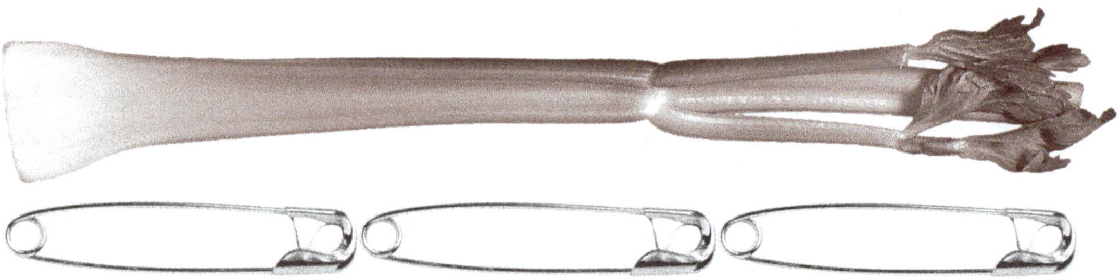

The celery stick is ☐ units long.

(d) 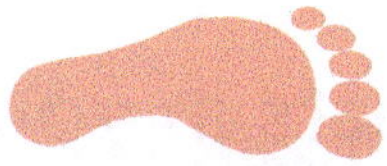 = 1 unit

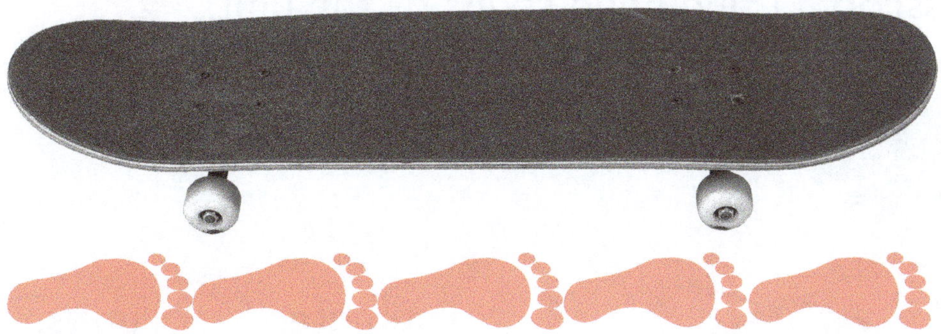

The skateboard is ☐ units long.

(e) 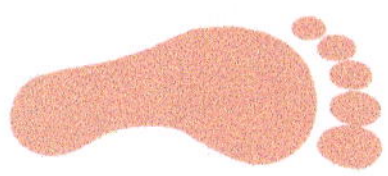 = 1 unit

The bicycle is ☐ units long.

2 Estimate and measure the length of objects in your classroom using hand spans as the unit.

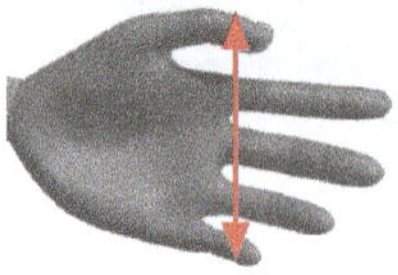 = 1 unit

(a) 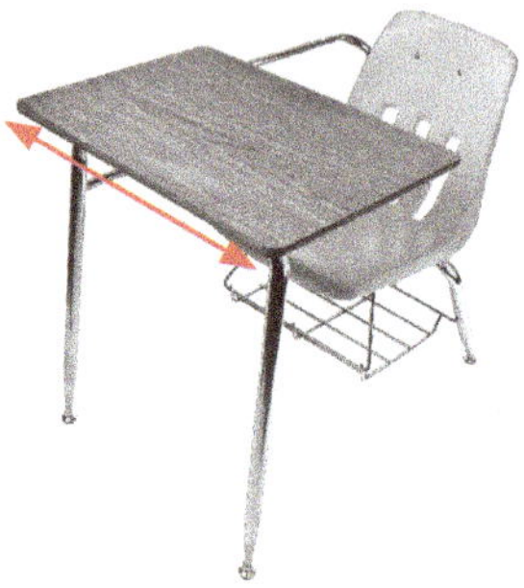

Estimate: ☐ units.

Actual measurement: ☐ units.

(b) 

Estimate: ☐ units.

Actual measurement: ☐ units.

(c) 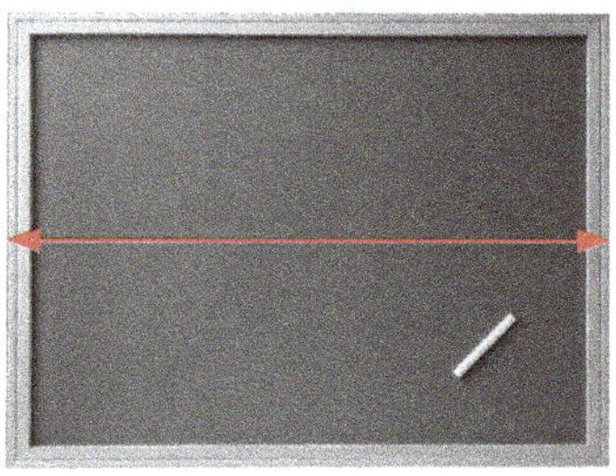

Estimate: ☐ units.

Actual measurement: ☐ units.

(d) 

Estimate: ☐ units.

Actual measurement: ☐ units.

3 Choose an object in your classroom to measure. Draw a picture of the object. Estimate the length in hand spans. Measure the length in hand spans.

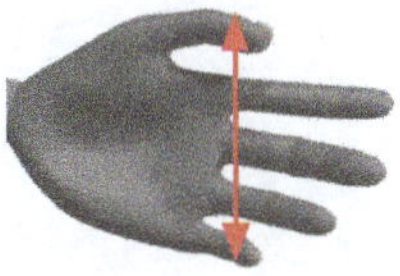 = 1 unit

Estimate: ☐ units.

Actual measurement: ☐ units.

Maths Scramble

Measure the lengths of the strips below to name the insect Samir has seen in the garden.

 = 1 unit

G

S

I

T

P			Y			
	9 units	2 units		5 units	7 units	4 units

1 unit	2 units	7 units	6 units	5 units	3 units

M

A

R

N

6 Mass

Practice 1: Comparing masses

1. Circle the heavier object.

(a)

(b)

(c)

(d)

2. Circle the lighter object.

(a)

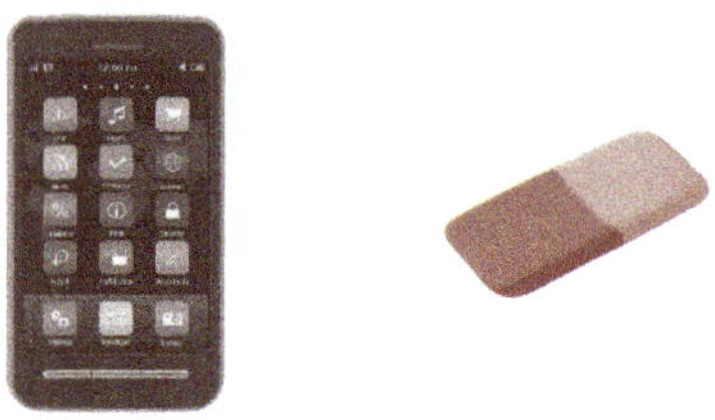

(b)

(c)

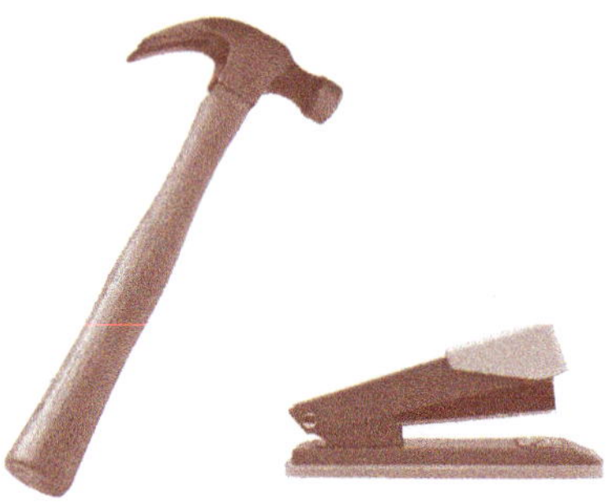

(d)

3 Use the words from the box to fill in the blanks.

heavier than	lighter than	as heavy as

(a)

The ball is ______ the box.

The box is ______ the ball.

(b)

The apple is ______ the carrot.

The carrot is ______ the apple.

(c)

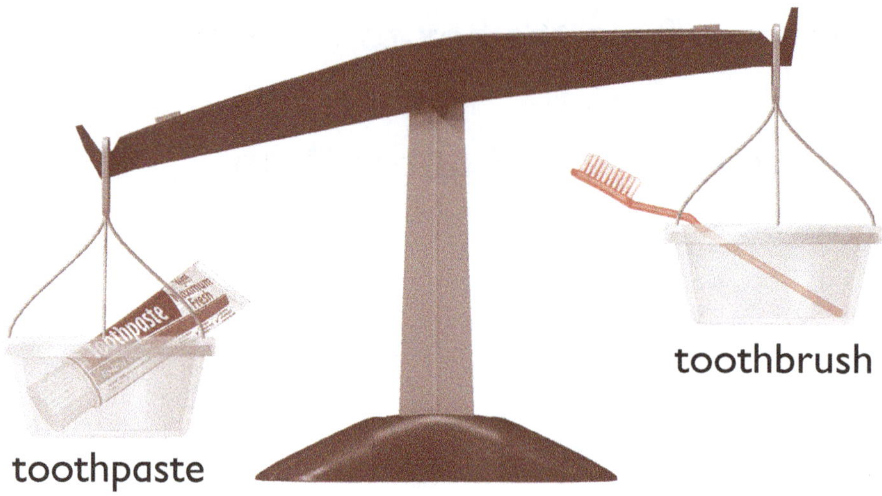

The toothpaste is ______ the toothbrush.

The toothbrush is ______ the toothpaste.

(d)

The scissors are ______ the toy car.

The toy car is ______ the scissors.

4 Fill in the blanks.

(a)

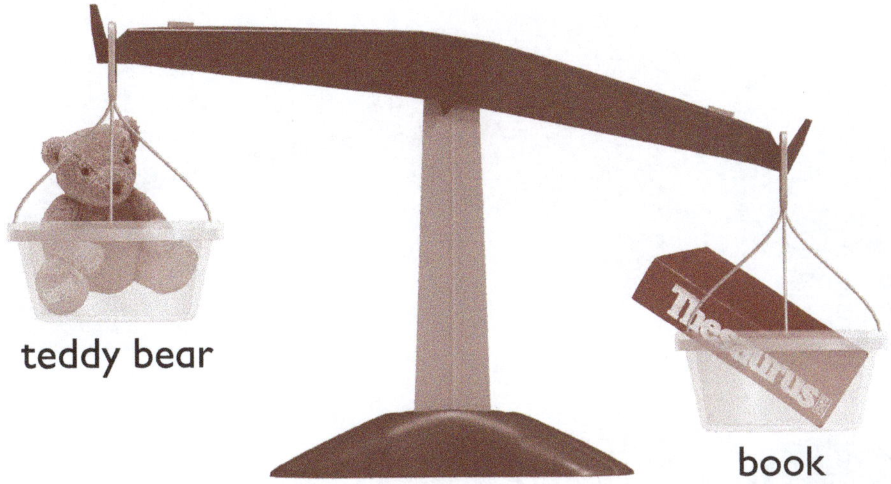

The ______ is heavier than the ______.

The ______ is lighter than the ______.

(b)

The ______ is heavier than the ______.

The ______ is lighter than the ______.

5 Draw the objects on the balance.

(a)

(b)

(c)

(d)

6 Circle the heaviest animal. Cross out the lightest animal.

(a)

(b)

7 Use the words from the box to fill in the blanks.

heavier	lighter	heaviest	lightest

(a)

The book is ______ than the scissors.

The book is ______ than the present.

The present is the ______.

The scissors are the ______.

(b)

The toy car is ________ than the pencil.

The toy car is ________ than the can.

The can is the ________.

The pencil is the ________.

8 Fill in the blanks.

The ______ is heavier than the mango.

The ______ is the lightest.

The ______ is the heaviest.

Problem Solving

The Max Maths team went shopping for food. Read the clues below and arrange the items from the lightest to the heaviest.

Item A

Item B

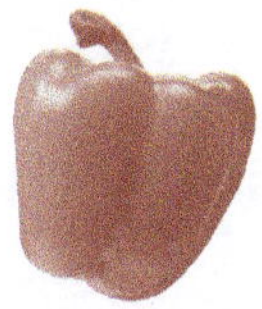

Item C

Item D

Item C is lighter than Item A.

Item B is heavier than Item A.

Item B is not the heaviest.

lightest → heaviest

Practice 2: Measuring mass

1. What is the mass of each object?

(a)

The mass of the mug is the same as ☐ cubes.

(b)

The mass of the potted plant is the same as ☐ cubes.

(c) Circle the correct word.

The potted plant is heavier / lighter than the mug.

2 What is the mass of the fruit?

(a)

The mass of the lemon is the same as ☐ .

(b)

The mass of the mango is the same as ☐ .

(c)

The mass of the orange is the same as ☐ .

(d) Arrange the fruits from the lightest to the heaviest.

☐ ☐ ☐

lightest → heaviest

3 Write the mass of each animal.

Then fill in the blanks on the next page.

(a)

The mass of the teddy is the same as ☐ marbles.

(b)

The mass of the toy rabbit is the same as ☐ marbles.

(c)

The mass of the doll is the same as ☐ marbles.

(d) The ________ is heavier than the teddy.

(e) The ________ is lighter than the teddy.

(f) The ________ is the lightest.

(g) The ________ is the heaviest.

Problem Solving

Arrange the food from the lightest to the heaviest.

lightest → heaviest

Practice 3: Measuring mass in units

1 What is the mass of each object?

Each stands for 1 unit.

(a)

The mass of the cup is ☐ units.

(b)

The mass of the pencil case is ☐ units.

(c)

The mass of the clock is ☐ units.

2 Each  stands for 1 unit.

Gift A

Gift B

Gift C

(a) The mass of Gift A is ___ units.

(b) The mass of Gift B is ___ units.

(c) The mass of Gift C is ___ units.

(d) Gift ___ is lighter than Gift A.

(e) Gift ___ is the heaviest.

(f) Gift ___ is the lightest.

7 Capacity

Practice 1: Comparing capacities

1 Draw a circle around the object that holds more.

(a)

(b)

(c)

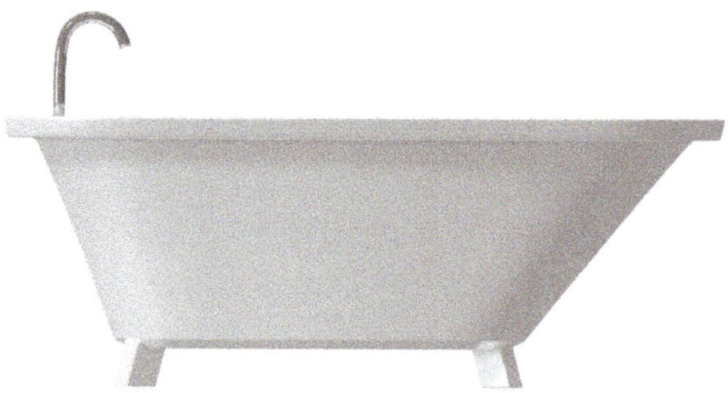

(d)

2 Draw a square around the object that holds less.

(a)

(b)

(c)

(d)

3 Draw around the object that is empty.

(a)

(b)

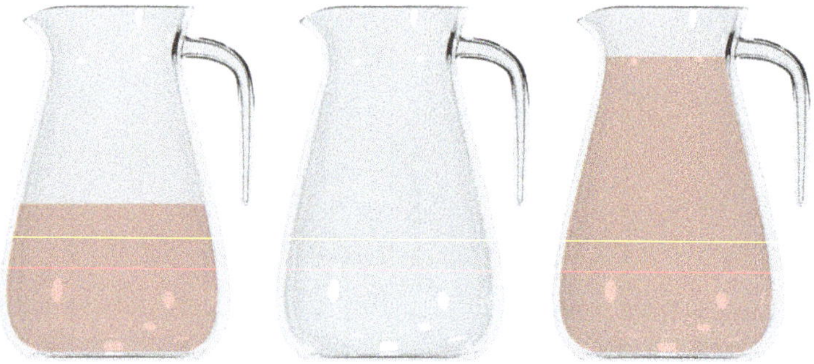

(c)

4 Draw around the object that is full.

(a)

(b)

(c)

5 Draw around the object that is half-full.

(a)

(b)

(c)

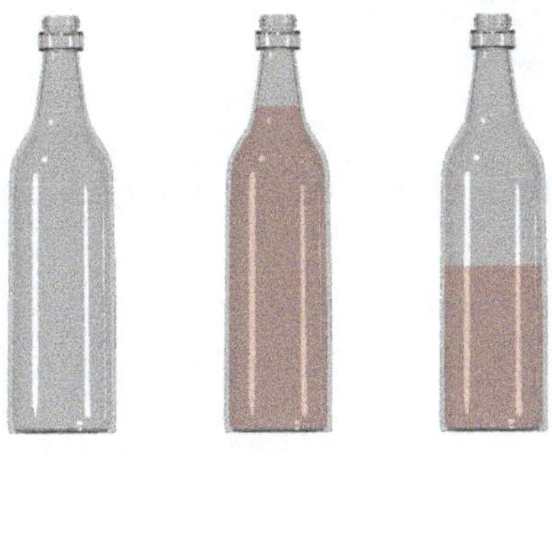

8 Time

Practice 1: Reading a clock

1. Complete the following.

   (a) Write the missing numbers on the clock face.

   (b) Draw the minute hand and the hour hand on the clock face to show 5 o'clock.

2 Label the hands of each clock as 'minute hand' or 'hour hand'.

(a)

(b)

(c)

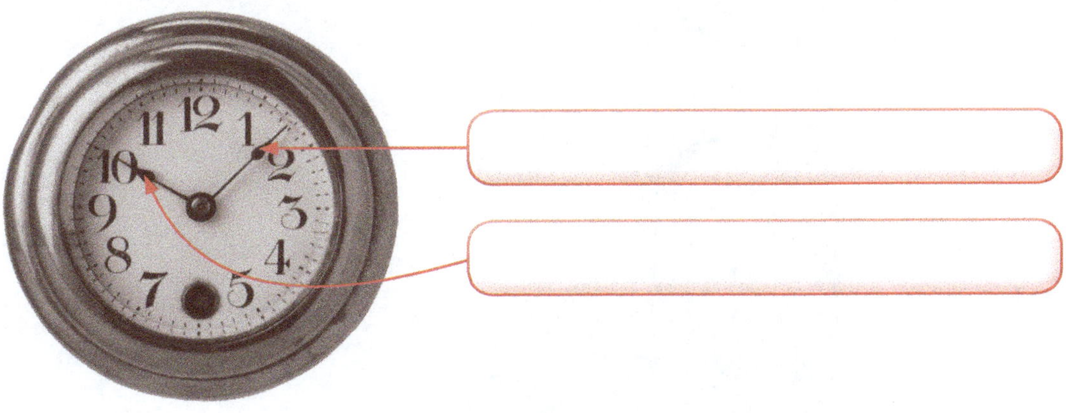

(d)

(e)

(f)

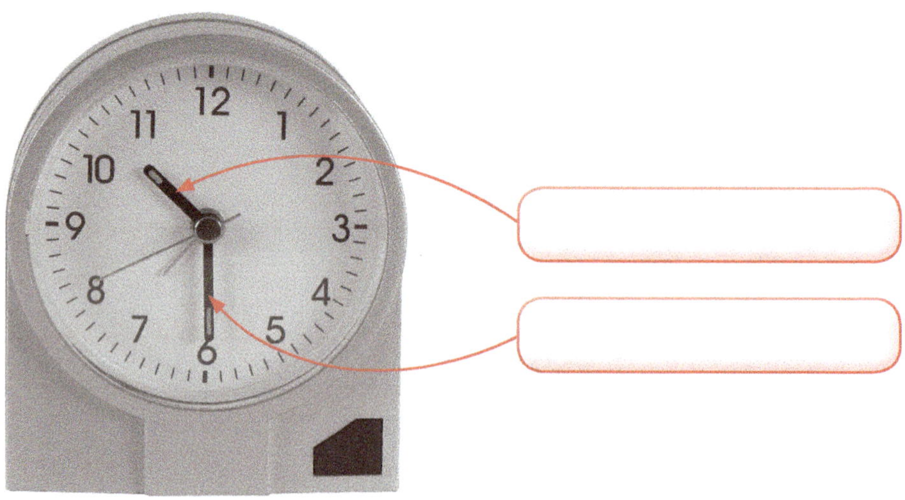

3 Look at how the time changes. Write how many hours have passed.

(a)

☐ hour has passed.

(b)

☐ hours have passed.

(c)

☐ hours have passed.

(d)

☐ hours have passed.

4 Look at the clock and complete the sentences.

(a)

The ______ hand is pointing at 12. The ______ hand is pointing at ___. The time is ___ o'clock.

(b)

The ______ hand is pointing at 12. The ______ hand is pointing at ___. The time is ___ o'clock.

(c)

The ______ hand is pointing at 12. The ______ hand is pointing at ___. The time is ___ o'clock.

Practice 2: Days of the week

1. Write the days of the week in order.

(a) ______ (b) ______

(c) ______ (d) ______

(e) ______ (f) ______

(g) ______

Practice 3: Months of the year

1. Write the months of the year in order.

(a) ______ (b) ______

(c) ______ (d) ______

(e) ______ (f) ______

(g) ______ (h) ______

(i) ______ (j) ______

(k) ______ (l) ______

9 Money

Practice 1: Coins

1. Match the coins to the correct amount of money.

• 50¢

• 1¢

• 5¢

• 20¢

• 10¢

• 2¢

2 Complete the table.

	10¢	
		50 cents
		5 cents
	20¢	

Practice 2: Exchanging money

1. Match the coins to the correct amount of money.

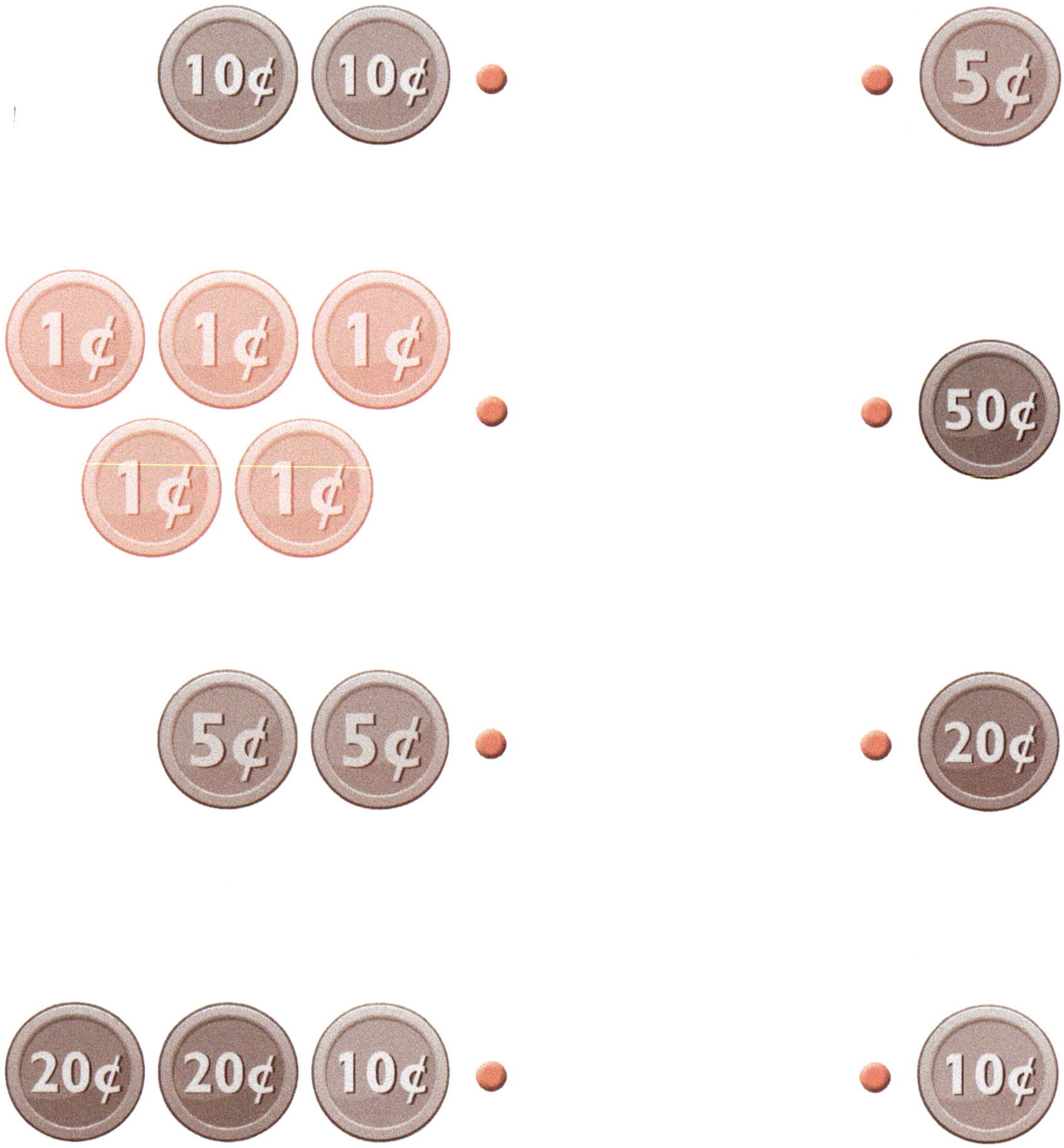

2 Colour the correct amount of money.

Example

20¢ = 10¢ 10¢ 5¢ 5¢

(a)

50¢ = 20¢ 10¢ 10¢ 10¢ 5¢ 5¢

(b)

20¢ = 10¢ 5¢ 5¢ 5¢ 2¢

(c)

5¢ = 20¢ 10¢ 2¢ 2¢ 1¢ 1¢

(d)

50¢ = 20¢ 10¢ 10¢ 5¢ 5¢ 2¢ 1¢

3 Count and write the correct amount of money.

Example

20¢ 10¢ 10¢ 10¢ 10¢ 10¢ | 70¢

(a) 50¢ 20¢ 10¢ 5¢ 5¢ | ______

(b) 20¢ 10¢ 5¢ 5¢ 5¢ 5¢ | ______

(c) 5¢ 5¢ 2¢ 2¢ 1¢ 1¢ | ______

(d) 20¢ 20¢ 10¢ 5¢ | ______

4 Write the fewest coins needed to buy each item.

Example

50¢	20¢	10¢	5¢	2¢	1¢
1		1			

(a)

50¢	20¢	10¢	5¢	2¢	1¢

(b)

50¢ 20¢ 10¢ 5¢ 2¢ 1¢

(c)

50¢ 20¢ 10¢ 5¢ 2¢ 1¢

(d)

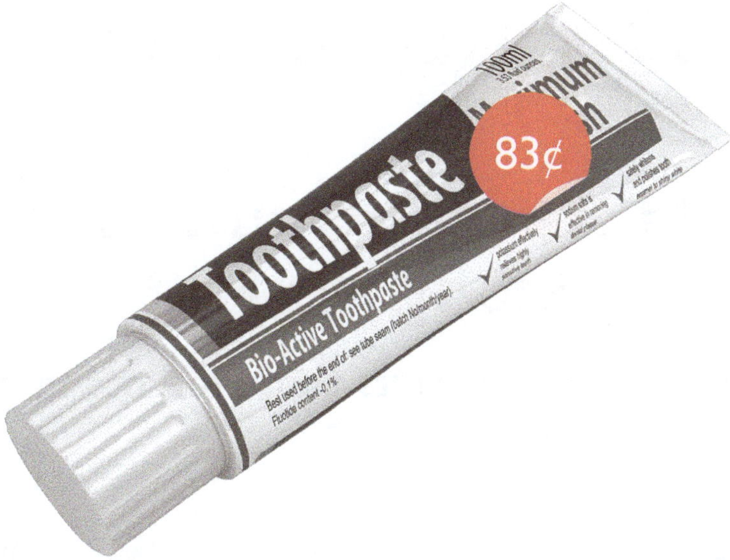

50¢ 20¢ 10¢ 5¢ 2¢ 1¢

(e)

50¢ 20¢ 10¢ 5¢ 2¢ 1¢

10 Data handling

Practice 1: Reading and making pictographs

1 The pictograph shows fruits that Han ate in a week.

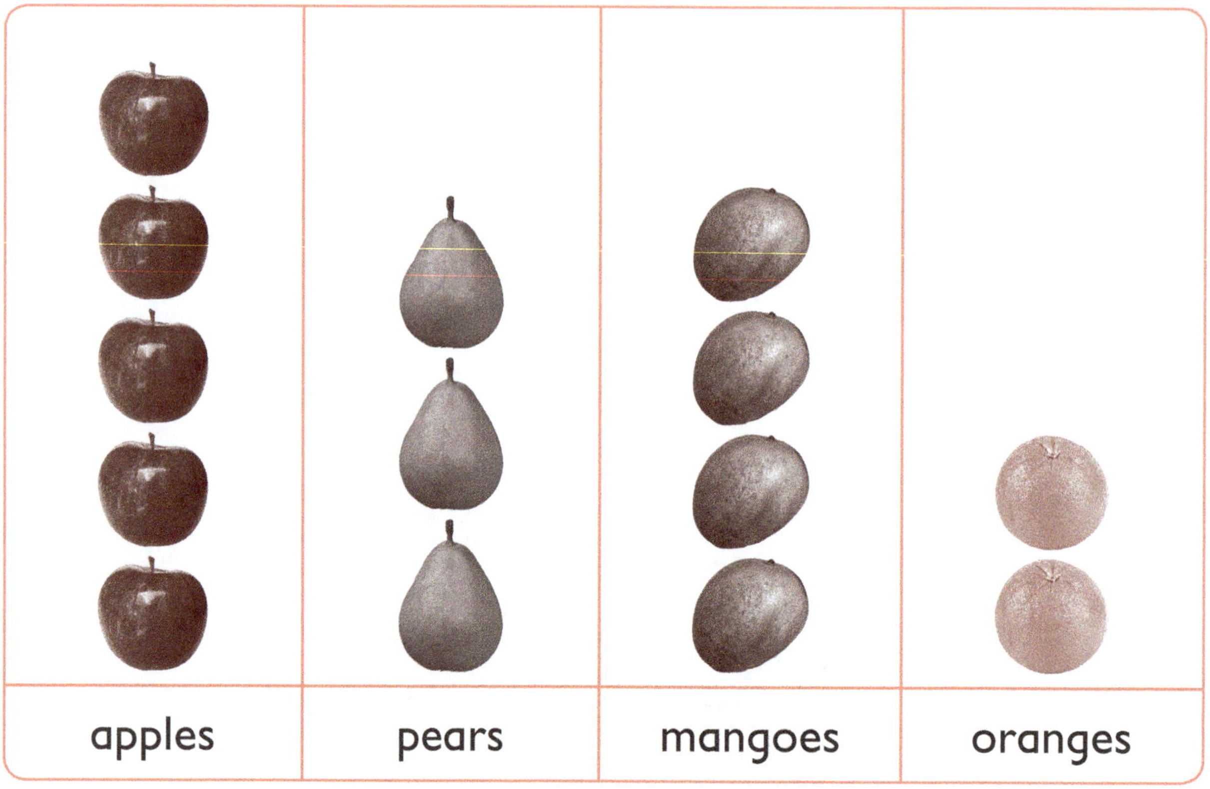

(a) Han ate ☐ apples.

(b) Han ate ☐ mangoes.

(c) Which fruit did Han eat the most? ☐

(d) Which fruit did Han eat the least? ☐

2 The pictograph below shows the items that Padma bought at the school bookshop.

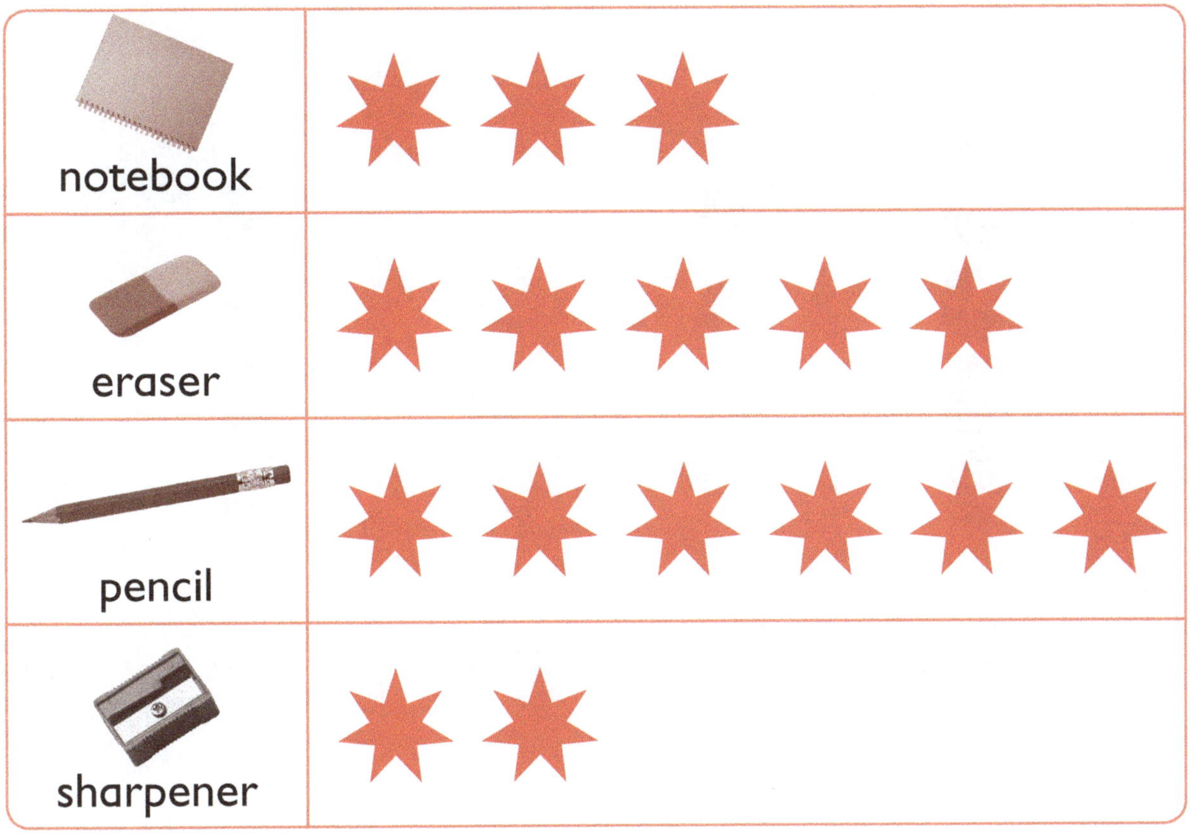

Each ★ stands for 1 item.

(a) How many erasers did Padma buy? ☐

(b) How many pencils did Padma buy? ☐

(c) Padma bought ☐ more erasers than notebooks.

(d) Padma bought ☐ fewer notebooks than pencils.

(e) Padma bought ☐ more pencils than sharpeners.

3 The pictograph below shows the number of children that were born in different months.

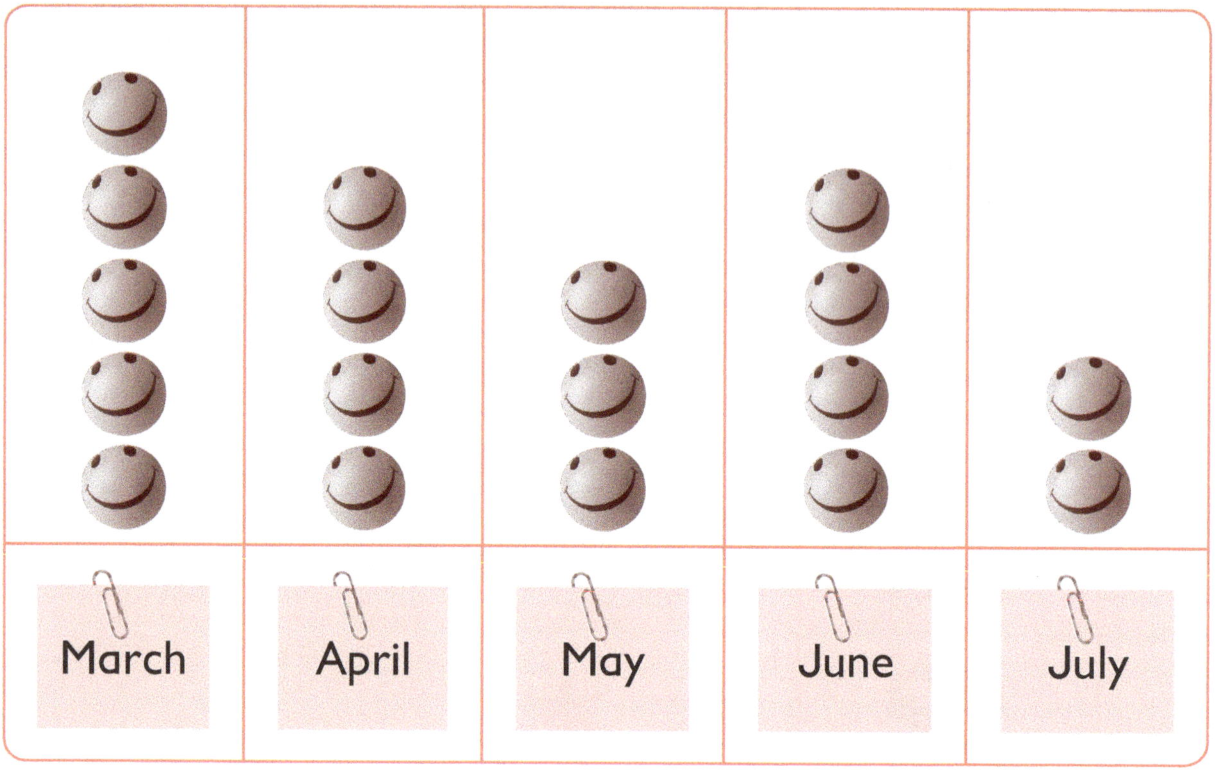

(a) In which month were the most children born? ☐

(b) In which month were the fewest children born? ☐

(c) How many children were born in April and May?

☐

(d) How many children were born in June and March?

☐

(e) There was ☐ more child born in May than in July.

4 The Max Maths team played a game of football. The pictograph below shows the number of goals they scored.

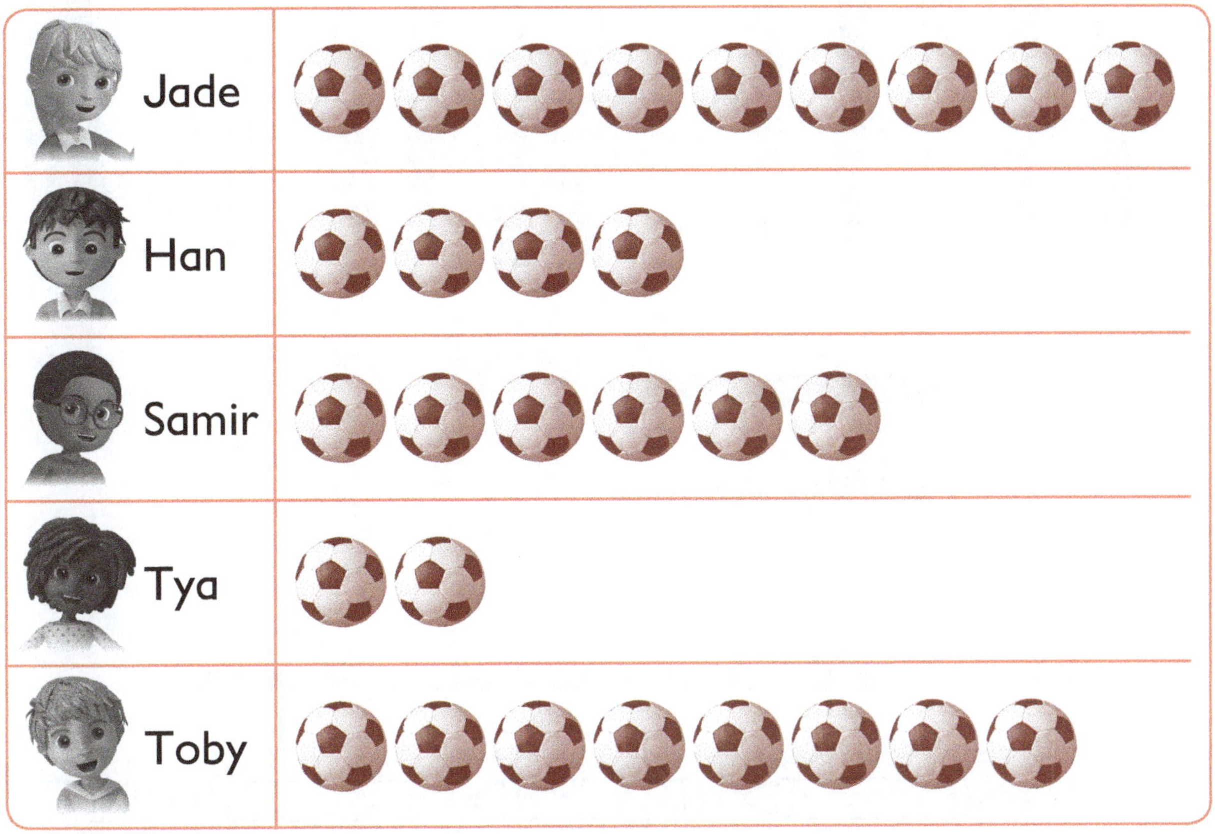

(a) Who scored the most goals? ______

(b) Who scored the fewest goals? ______

(c) Han scored more goals than ______.

(d) Samir scored ______ more goals than Tya.

(e) Tya scored ______ fewer goals than Toby.

(f) Toby and Samir scored ______ goals altogether.

5 **(a)** Count the crayons in Toby's pencil case.

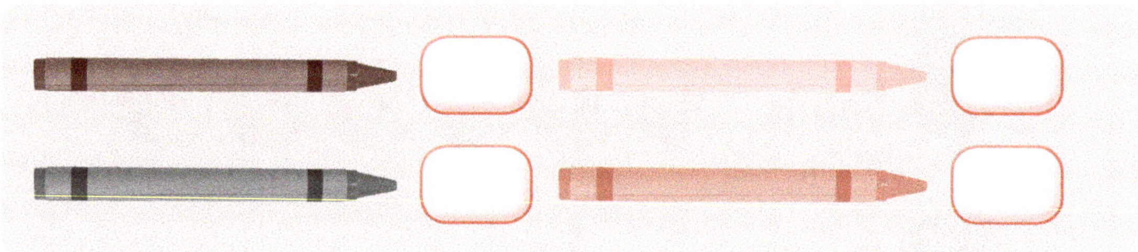

(b) Colour the crayons to make a pictograph.

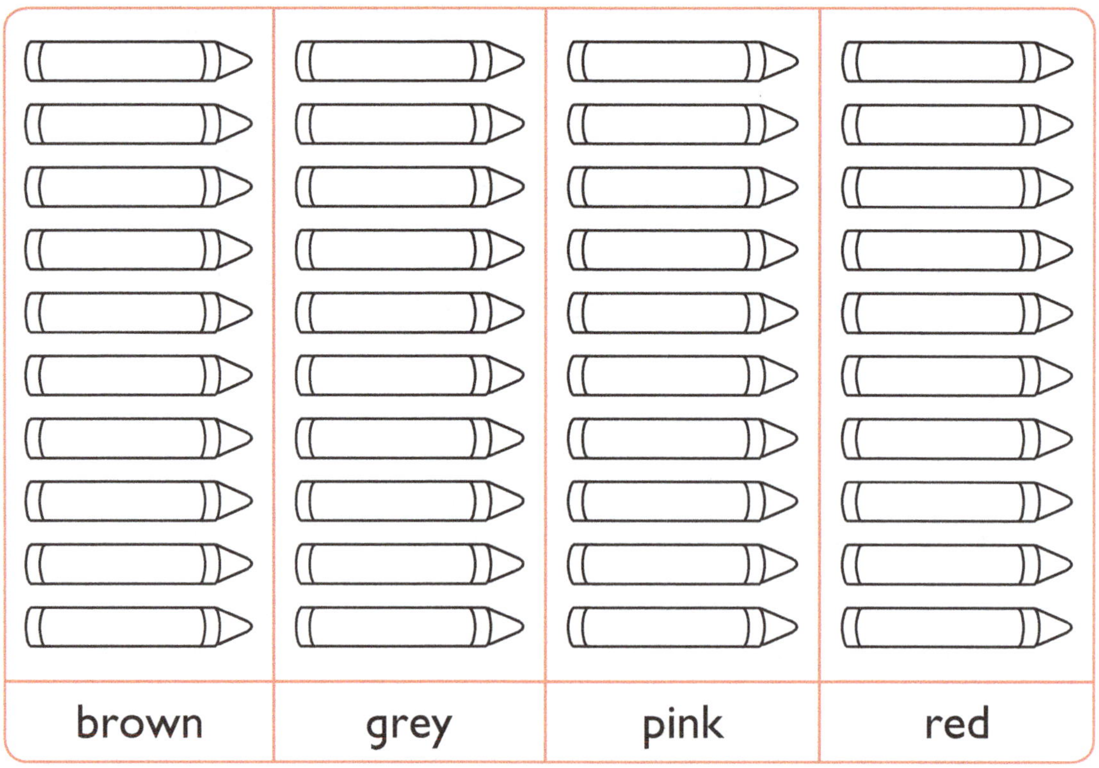

6 Samir rolled a dice many times. Use the pictures below to make a pictograph.

Each ● stands for 1 dice roll.

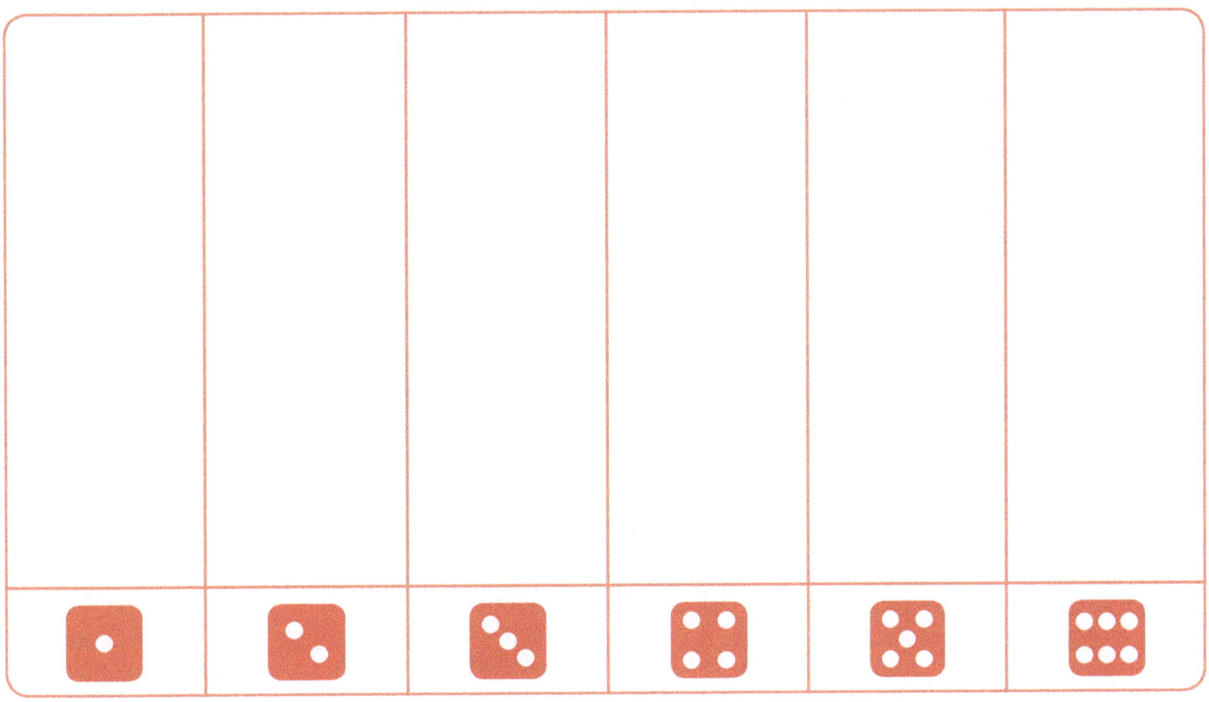

(a) Samir rolled ☐ the most number of times.

(b) Samir rolled ☐ the least number of times.

(c) Samir rolled 4 more  than he rolled ☐.

(d) Samir rolled 3 fewer  than he rolled ☐.

7 Tya and Han visited a garden.
Make a pictograph of the flowers they saw.

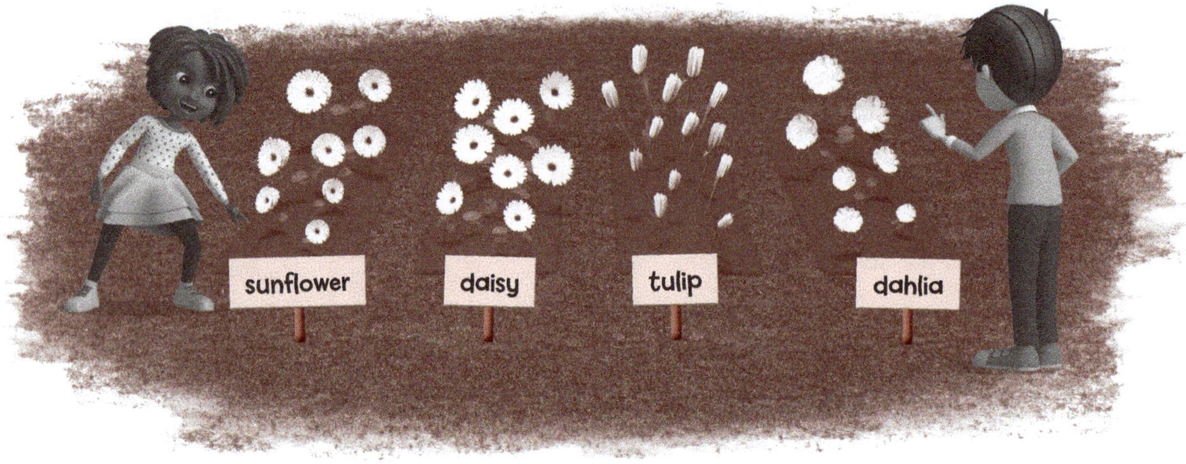

Each stands for 1 flower.

sunflowers	daisies	tulips	dahlias

(a) There are ☐ more tulips than sunflowers.

(b) There are ☐ fewer dahlias than tulips.

(c) There are ☐ sunflowers and daisies altogether.

8 Samir and Tya also spotted some creatures in the garden. Here is what they spotted.

2 butterflies | 5 ladybirds | 6 snails | 1 lizard

Samir and Tya both made pictographs to show the creatures they spotted. One of the pictographs is incorrect.

Each ● stands for 1 animal.

Samir's pictograph

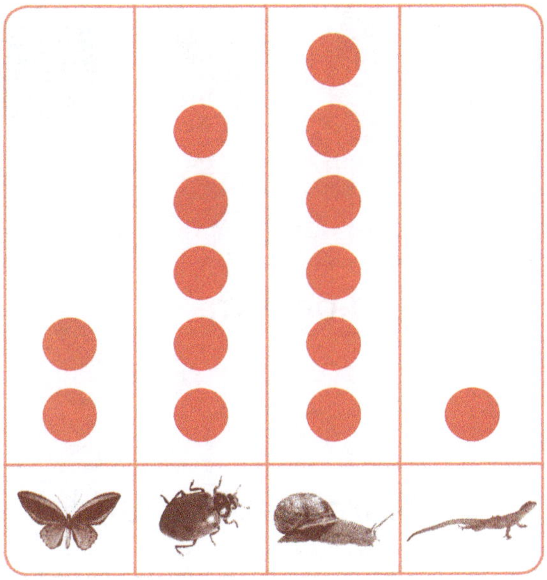

Tya's pictograph

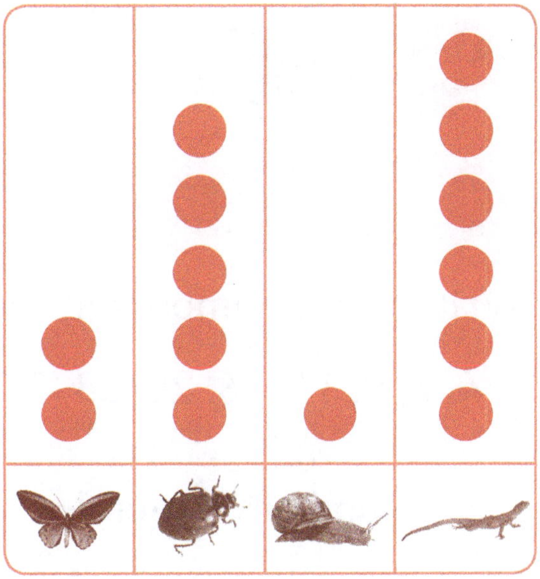

(a) Whose pictograph is correct? ______________

(b) Why is the other pictograph incorrect?

____

Practice 2: Reading Venn and Carroll diagrams

1. Draw an arrow showing where each shape belongs in the Venn diagram.

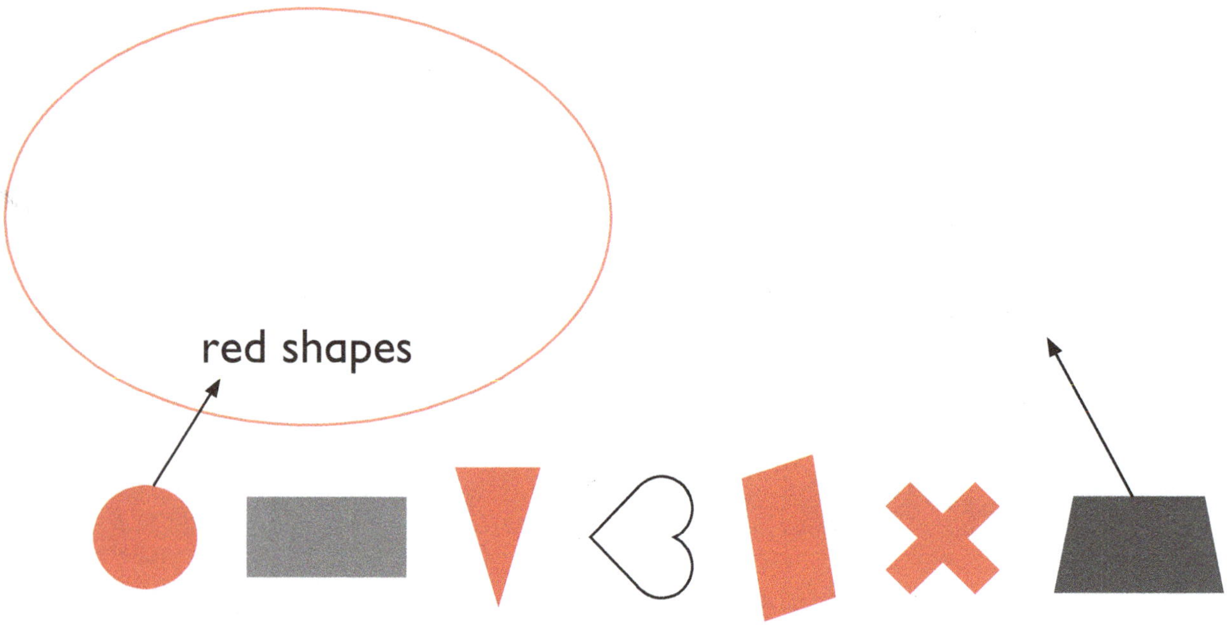

2. Write these numbers in the Carroll diagram.

1, 4, 7, 9, 11, 16, 20, 23, 27

Numbers under 15	Numbers not under 15